THE SURFER'S GUIDE
to
BAJA

By Mike Parise

Cover Art by Bob Towner

Maps by Cricket

4th Edition

SurfPress Publishing, California

www.TheSurfersGuides.com

THE SURFER'S GUIDE TO BAJA

By Mike Parise

Published by:
SurfPress Publishing
P.O. Box 492342
Los Angeles, CA 90049

Copyright © 2012 by Michael Parise
First Printing 2001
Printed in the United States of America

Library of Congress Cataloging-in-Publication Data
Parise, Michael
        The Surfer's Guide to Baja/ by Michael Parise. — 4th ed.
        p. cm.
        Includes index
        ISBN-13: 978-0-967910055
        ISBN-10: 0967910056
        1. Baja California—Guidebooks. I. Title.
        2. Surfing

To Roman

"Motel Chavez, Motel Chavez…"

Baja Norte

U.S.A.

MEXICO

Tijuana Sloughs
Playas de Tijuana
Baja Malibu
Rosarito Beach
Calafia
K-38
Las Gaviotas
K-55
La Fonda

Tijuana

Rosarito

Salsipuedes
San Miguel
Islas de
Todos Santos

Ensenada

Boca de Santo Tomás
Punta San José

Punta Cabras
Punta San Isidro

San Antonio del Mar

Cabo Colonet

Quatro Casas (Punta San Telmo)
Freighters (Punta San Jacinto)
Punta Camalú
Playas San Ramón

San Quintín

Sea of Cortez

Cabo San Quintín
Playa Santa Maria
El Socorro
Casas
Punta Baja

El Rosario

1

Punta San Antonio
Punta San Fernando
Punta San Carlos

Punta Canoas
Puerto Canoas

Punta Blanca
Punta Cono
Punta Maria
Punta Lobos/Punta Ositos
Punta Prieta/Punta Negra
Punta Rocosa
Punta Santa Rosalillita
Punta Rosarito/The Wall
Miller's Landing

Pacific Ocean

Baja Sur

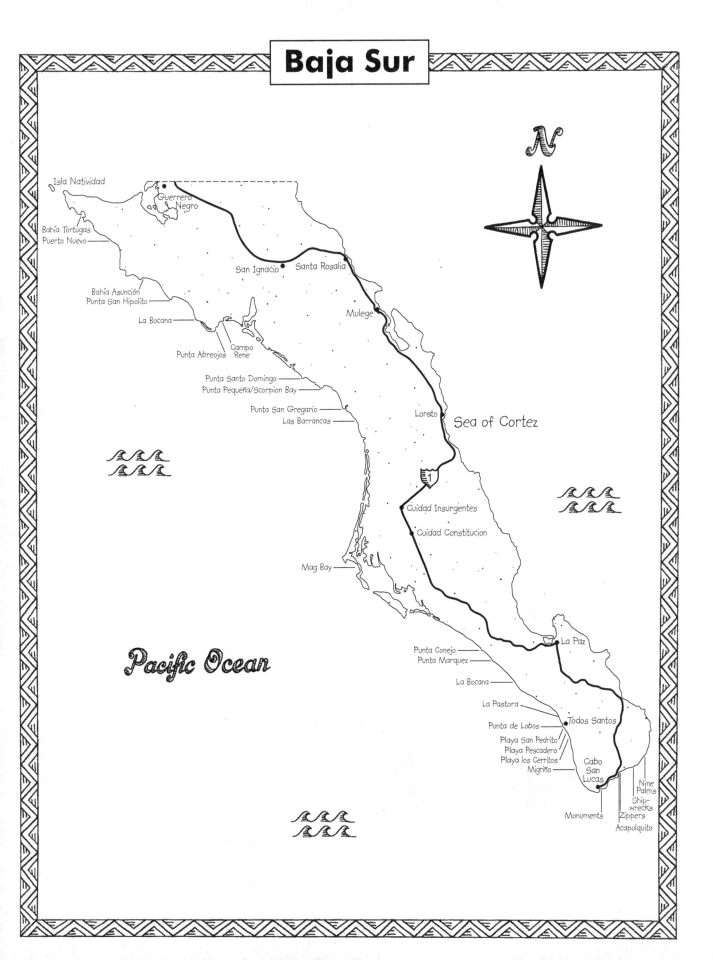

TABLE OF CONTENTS

INTRODUCTION

" **I**'d traveled all over the world, and I eventually came to realize that I hadn't even surfed some of the spots you can drive to from my house."

- Brian Conley, *The Surfer's Journal*, Volume 16, #4

When crossing the Mexican border for your first time you will likely experience feelings of apprehension. Hell, the apprehension probably started the day you decided to go. We've all been there. In that very moment of lining up between the cement lane barriers and passing from San Ysidro to Tijuana what was once rabid anticipation of a surf trip switches to trepidation, as visions of drug executions, Federales, Montezuma's Revenge, sharks, barren deserts, bodies melting in barrels of acid and filthy jails replace fantasies of perfect, offshore-groomed barrels. It is just a blip, however, caused by the jolt from confronting this Third World country for the first time. It is a jolt that conjures up recollections of rumors, news articles and the horror stories of trips gone bad. Then, after 10 minutes or so of smelling new unpleasant smells winding through Tijuana traffic you find yourself looking out at *Oceano Pacifico*, measuring every sea hump for surf potential and once again anticipating the joys that can only be found via a real surf adventure.

All that imagery is interesting, of course, but you bought this guide to prep for surf travel. So to set expectations now that you have plunked down three days' lunch money, herein you will find information on how to get the most and best surf out of Baja, and not much more. To learn more about Baja's colorful history and other subjects of general travel interest, you need to get a real travel guide, like Moon Handbook's *Baja, Tijuana to Cabo San Lucas* by Nikki Goth Itoi (the best and only guide book you'll need), because there is not much here about anything not related to the pursuit of surf.

If you have been surfing for awhile, you know that surf travel has changed dramatically. It wasn't that long ago that nearly all surf travel was adventure. There were no packaged surf tours. No luxury yachts with chefs, air conditioned cabins, massages and entertainment centers. No surf resorts with pop-out board rentals and surf schools. And no English-speaking party guide to meet you at the airport, strap your board bags on the roof and seal you in an air-conditioned van to protect you from the locals until your crew is delivered to the surf "camp", mojitos waiting on the bar and flowers on your bed. The magazines weren't filled with articles on fantasy surf travel. No surf cams previewing exactly what you could expect at breaks thousands of miles away. No surf forecasts. All there was was *The Surf Report* with a few pages of basic but vital information and one or two photos, some unidentified clips in videos, word-of-mouth, and a few dog-eared pages torn from long-lost surf mags.

That old-school adventure lives just over the California border in Baja. From that trip through Tijuana to that last right point around the East Cape, it's more adventure than not. Except for a half-dozen guidebooks or so, and a ton of scattered info on the Internet, Baja has been bypassed by the surf travel industry in favor of the more expensive trips with higher markups and surf media support fears, and in some ways that's good. Sure, Baja has changed and will keep changing, but not much, and for some reason it's just not as exciting to the surf travel world as many destinations. So there are still no boat trips to Isla Cresciente or the East Cape and the packaged trips involve sleeping bags, cold showers and no a/c. Baja remains a gritty experience, one that can still resemble surf travel of days gone by.

Back to the guide…Baja, which is really Baja California, is divided into two states, *Baja California Norte* (Northern Baja) and *Baja California Sur* (Southern Baja), with the division at the 28th Parallel just north of Guerrero Negro. How this guide is further distinguishes Baja's various regions has more to do with states of mind, and perhaps psychological driving barriers, than latitude lines or governmental borders. So this guide may not match up well with other travel guides, but it should make sense once you've made the drive.

While this humble writer has done a fair amount of time in Baja, like *Wayne's World's* host Wayne Campbell said, "I'm not worthy." I haven't camped for months at a time on a deserted point, hours off the highway, accepting gifts of soap, wax and toilet paper from the occasional visitor. I don't have a quiver of broken boards brought back to usefulness with boat resin and panga-weight glass. And I have never seen the inside of a Mexican jail. For those reasons and more, there are dozens if not hundreds of surfers who should have written this guide before or instead of me, as they know Baja things I'll never know. But for the surfer who has never been to Baja, or the occasional visitor, I am certain this guide will be a big help. That, I've been told many times over.

Occasionally I am also told how I skipped a spot or three. Or that I should have given directions to one of the less-visited spots. Those observations are often correct. Out of respect for those who have paid and continue to pay enormous dues, and in keeping with SurfPress' credo, no secret spots are revealed in these pages. And "secret" means that the spot hasn't been written up elsewhere before. There are no photos either (this is not a coffee table book), and precise directions to the more out-of-the-way spots are left to the truly dedicated. So while over 120 spots are described herein, many with turn-by-turn directions, they are spots previously publicized elsewhere. That makes this guide a compilation, with added depth crafted from firsthand experience and other research. For those who believe this book will ruin Baja by revealing their favorite, uncrowded, undiscovered breaks: Relax, it won't. Besides, there is the Internet for that. And frankly, there are more talkers than takers.

In one respect it would be good if this guide gets more surfers to Baja. A string of Baja's best breaks have been facing extinction, and some are already gone, as just like California Norte before, boat harbors replace surf breaks. The Department of Mexican Tourism (Fonatur) approved and funded a plan (*Escalera Nautica*) to build a chain of over 20 boat harbors covering the entire coastline of Baja and extending to the mainland. Tourists were expected travel Baja from the water instead of the land. Surf breaks included in the plan included Abreojos, Scorpion Bay, Punta Rosalillita (already done) and more. Had enough surfers traveled to these breaks over the years the dollars would have come to build local economies and prevent this foolish endeavor. Fortunately, that plan failed after losing just one break, but more surf is at risk, and surf-tourism dollars talk.

With or without those incredible, endangered breaks, the vast majority of Baja is still unsurfed. The spots have been mapped for years, but most surfers just don't make the effort to travel much beyond Ensenada's horribly crowded San Miguel. I can't tell you how many times I have driven up to perfect point breaks that everyone knows only to see an empty lineup. Even spots like K-38, a well-known and easily accessible break just south of the border is crazy crowded on weekends but empties on Mondays. The fact is, most of Baja is unsurfed most of the time, and it will stay that way for awhile.

OK, enough jibber-jabber about this guidebook. Get yourself ready for some surf adventure, mixed with dust, tequila, fresh corn tortillas, lobster, garbage, teenage soldiers with AK-47s, roadside shrines, toothy smiles, tittie dogs, diarrhea, moonscapes, bitter expats, Tecate with a lime, ceviche with more lime tons of totally uncrowded surf there for the taking. It is all yours. Just go.

Vamos amigos!

BACKGROUND AND TIPS

Respect

You have heard it before and you will hear it again: The best tip to give a traveling surfer is to show respect. Respect the locals, respect the land and respect your fellow traveling surfers. And when it comes to Baja, you will probably figure this out on your own pretty quickly, as this is one crazy place.

Respect and don't *expect*. Don't expect what you get back home. Don't expect to have every little want satisfied. They don't always have what you want. This is not your country, and they know it.

Show respect in how you communicate. If you didn't already know, they speak Spanish in Mexico. Don't expect anyone to speak English. Even if you have never had a Spanish class you should try to speak Spanish. It is not that difficult. You already know more than you think. *Gracias. Por Favor. Hola. Adios. Cerveza. Tequila. Los Angeles. San Diego. San Francisco.* See, it's easy. And it's a great way to show respect—not expecting the locals to understand your language. You are the foreigner now. It is their turf and you are just a visitor. And in the surf you're an uninvited visitor. Their country. Their laws. Their language. Their surf.

The Land

You've probably heard of the Baja 1000 off-road race. It runs from Ensenada to La Paz, or about 1,000 miles. Since Ensenada is below the northern border and La Paz is above the southern tip that means there is well over 1,000 miles of coast, or over 1,000 miles of surf potential.

Baja is mostly desert—rocks, mountains, *arroyos* and desert. It does get tropical in a few places at the southern end around Cabo during the summer and early fall (hurricane season) when warm, wet weather moves up from the waters off Central America (*Chubascos*), and there are a few other swampy lagoons here and there. But for the most part, it's dry—rocks, mountains and desert.

Climate

While Baja is mostly desert, it does rain. It rains during the winter in the north, coming from the southern edges of the same storm systems that pass through the U.S. Almost all of that rain falls from December to March. From Ensenada to Bahía Magdalena the rainfall rate drops by over half to just a few inches a year. Despite that, it's enough to cause flash floods, axle-sucking mud pits, and spitting rivermouth barrels.

Rainfall picks up again in the south near the Cape, coming from the northern edges of tropical storms and hurricanes originating off the west coast of mainland Mexico south of Puerto Vallarta, some of which hit Cabo head-on. The rain comes from June to October, peaking July through September. (By the way, Baja roads don't handle rain well. The roads are not well-engineered, so they don't always disperse the water. And once off the main highway, most of the roads aren't paved, so even four-wheel drive vehicles often find themselves stranded when visiting the wrong places at the wrong times.)

While deserts are known as outdoor ovens, Baja just is not that hot, especially near the ocean. Temperatures in the north near the ocean average from 60 degrees to 75 degreesF (Celsius 16 to 24) year-round, cooled by the California Current. California's infamous "June Gloom" — the coastal fog seen in early summer — hits Northern Baja as well, mostly from May to July.

The Central Desert area from El Rosario south to San Ignacio can get hot where it often goes well over 100 degrees, and it cools off a lot at night. But don't let the high inland temperatures fool you. Near the ocean it's nearly always cool to chilly to downright cold, so bring a sweatshirt and a jacket.

The Cabo area also gets hot, but not as hot as the Central Desert, and it's humid in the summer as this is the Tropics. In the winter and spring it can get pretty chilly on the West Cape, especially at night, so bring something warm to wear. (In fact, the entire Pacific Coast cools at night, so always bring something warm to wear at night, like a sweatshirt, no matter where you go.) The East Cape rarely drops below 60 degrees, and only at night. Typically, temperatures average in the 80s in the early spring and late fall, and climb up to 100 in July and August.

Water Temperatures

Since there is a coastline of over 1,000 miles, there is also a range of water temperatures. Let's break this down to north and south and explore.

First the bad news: Northern Baja water is cold nearly all year. This comes as a surprise to most the first time they hear or experience this. After all, Mexico is south of California and is mostly desert, right? Just look at those Corona commercials. Does that water look cold? No, it doesn't, but the water is colder than California nonetheless. I could explain it (California Current, one of the five major coastal currents in the world, this one running north to south, starting in British Columbia and bringing cold water down, but also having major upwelling, another cause for cold water), or just tell you to bring a 2/2 and a springsuit in the late summer, a 3/2 in fall, and a 4/3 and booties in the winter and spring. And for the big surf on the island of Todos Santos add a hood. At its balmiest, which is usually around September, some spots in Northern Baja can get warm enough to trunk it, up to a bit over 70 degrees in a really good year, but springsuits or shortjohns are usually in order. In the winter and spring the water temp gets down to the mid-to-low fifties. Spring, the windiest time of the year usually has the coldest water. If you are heading to the area between Punta Banda and the Seven Sisters, expect the water to be five to ten degrees colder than the surrounding areas due to upwelling from the everpresent wind. Cabo Colonet, for example, can dip into the 50s in the summer. Lastly, the offshores around the Seven Sisters do a good job of blowing the warmer water out to sea, so expect it to be especially cold there.

Now the good news: Southern Baja is mostly warm, all the way in the south that is. From Bahía Tortugas south to the West Cape, the water temperature maxes out at about 75 degrees in the summer, but even this far south it can drop into to the low 50s in the winter or spring, depending on where you are headed. (Well, yes it does get cold.) Cabo stays pretty warm, typically above 70 degrees, and sometimes well over 80 degrees, but drops into the upper 60s in the spring. The East Cape ranges from 65 degrees to the mid-80s, which is almost too warm, if that's possible. In general, the West Cape is usually about five degrees colder than the Cabo San Lucas/San José del Cabo "Corridor". If heading to the Cabo area, bring a variety of rubber to cover yourself from the West to East Capes, probably a springsuit for the West Cape down to a rashguard for the Corridor and East Cape. You never know when you might need a wetsuit down there. I surfed Zippers one June in a springsuit, and I was glad I brought it. The next year I surfed Zippers in July and the water was *too* warm.

It is difficult to get reports on water temperatures outside the U.S. A few places to find up-to-date water temperatures include Surfline.com, MagicSeaweed.com, ssec.wisc.edu, Bajainsider.com and Surf-Forecast.com.

When to Go

How about now? Baja is a year-round surf destination. The West Coast catches swell for much of its length all year, except those parts most shadowed from the NW by the Vizcaíno Peninsula. The southern tip is best from spring through fall when the Southern Hemisphere and hurricane *(Chubascos)* swells are working best. The only time of year when you might think twice about going is during the spring when it gets pretty windy and the water gets colder, really cold in the north. Some guys plan their Cabo trips around hurricanes, hoping to hit it just right and catch the swells as they wrap around into the East Cape points and reefs. Great plan, but there is also the risk of actually getting caught in a hurricane or at least some heavy tropical rains complete with mudslides and flash floods. Not all bad, though, as the run-off from those same tropical rains creates some epic sandbars. (Wait a bit after the rain, as the runoff can be disease-ridden.)

Monthly Average Wave Face Heights

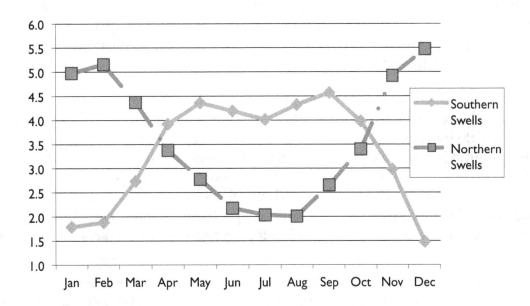

Data Source: Compiled from Surfline/Wavetrak (www.surfline.com)

Tides

Tide charts are easier to find than water temperature reports, which kinda sucks as you can figure out the tides when you get there. The only way to really figure out the water temp is to get in. Anyhow, if you haven't figured it out yet, go to Surfline.com, MagicSeaweed.com or WetSand.com for good tide charts. Then there is the techie-ish site: http://tbone.biol.sc.edu/tide/sitesel.html. (Be sure to click through to the "Alphabetical list of all tidal height sites".) You will find a handful of Baja tide charts, but none for Cabo.

Time Zones

Baja Norte stays on the same time as California all year, Pacific Standard Time, from the last Sunday in October to the first Sunday in April, and Pacific Daylight Time the remainder. Baja Sur is aligned with Mountain Standard Time.

What to Pack

If you are like most, the last day before you leave on a surf trip is spent in a nervous, anxious state. This is due to the anticipation of good, uncrowded surf, of course, but the hurry to get last-minute chores finished so you can leave with a clear conscience (rarely possible) is a big influence, too. There is also the only fear worse than a pintail-first sucking over the falls: forgetting to pack something (like fins).

Deciding what to pack for Baja depends on the type of trip you are planning. Are you camping at The Wall or stylin' it in a Cabo resort? Flying straight to Natividad or driving from Playas de Tijuana to Punta Perfecta? For most, Baja is a road trip, but whichever it's, here's a long list covering most everything, albeit not enough for a proper camping trip and too much for a Cabo weekend.

- **Airline tickets**: Or more likely a hard copy of your receipt from your online booking. (This assumes, of course, that you are flying, and that is likely to Cabo.) Do not put your tickets away at all or you will forget them. Sometimes I carry mine around in my backpack for a week before I go just to make sure I don't forget them. Or tape them to your surfboard—you won't forget that. As of this writing – early 2012 – don't bother with the electronic boarding passes. They are still unreliable so it just adds another travel problem. Besides, your hard copy printout converts to a handy piece of notepaper shortly after takeoff. And when on the road, handy notepaper is always, um, handy.

- **Passport**: Absolutely required. Prior to 2007 passports were not required for trips under 72 hours. That changed. Minors (under 18 years of age) going to Mexico without a parent need to get a notarized consent form signed by one or both parents. Forms are available at Mexican consulates or www.Free-Legal-Document.com.

- **Tourist Cards and Visas**: A passport is not enough for anyone planning to spend over 72 hours in Mexico or heading south of Ensenada.

  A Mexican Tourist Card or FM-T (Migratory Form for Foreign Tourist or *Forma Migratoria Para Tourista*) is required if you will be in Baja more than three days (but less than 180) or if traveling south of Ensenada. FMM tourist visas (good for 180 days) are required if you want to fish in Mexico. Visas are required for stays of over 180 days. Visas can be obtained at the Mexican auto insurance offices, some travel agencies (such as Discover Baja), Mexican Consulates (see Appendix) the Mexican National Tourist Council and at the border crossings, airports and ports. One easy place to pick up a Tourist Card is just as you cross the border at Tijuana in the Declaration Area to the right of the entry. To get one you will need to show the authorities your passport.

It doesn't end there. You'll need to get it validated once in Mexico. At the San Ysidro (San Diego) crossing get it validated just as you cross the border into Tijuana at the secondary inspection area (simply pull over to the right and ask). Or head to Ensenada to the office of the *Delegacíon de Servicios Migratórios* (immigration office—another good place to pick up a visa) which is on your left on Highway 1-D just as you pull into town (do not take the bypass).

If flying in on a commercial airline, they will provide the Tourist Card and it will get stamped upon arrival.

As mentioned, your Tourist Card will be valid for 180 days, but it can be renewed or extended. For extensions apply at the *Servicios Migratórios,* which has offices in most cities and towns. Not that you would, but don't bother going for an extension until your card is about to expire as they will not give it until you really need it, and no one knows how that is determined. There is another kind of visa, the *Visitante Rentista,* or FM-3, which is good for longer stays, but this book is for travelers, not movers.

You may be asked to show your tourist papers at highway checkpoints, so have them ready. Always expect some sort of difficulty, so be patient and respectful. Your impatience or efficiency standards are of no concern to anyone in Mexico.

- **Surfboards**: Ah, the big question. Which boards? Bring as many as feasible or convenient. If it's a quick fly-in to Cabo, one board is the call as the inconvenience of packing and carrying extra boards grows exponentially with each board, and some airlines charge for each board. Otherwise, bring two or more, for lots of reasons. It's a fact of life that boards get trashed in travel, so you may decide to carry a second simply as backup. But there are better reasons, and they could depend on whether you are a shortboarder, longboarder, or both.

Shortboarders heading to Baja Norte might consider bringing a bigger board than usual – a step-up. The waves are typically bigger and juicer in Baja than its closest neighbor, Southern California, and the water is colder, so the extra volume can be welcome. Shortboarders heading to Baja Sur should probably just bring their everyday boards.

The same probably goes for longboarders, although most are happy to bring one for all occasions. Even if you mostly shortboard, you may want to bring a longboard to take advantage of the long points in Baja Sur on the smaller days.

Now, if you have *huevos grandes*, you will want to bring a step-up or a gun for the bigger, juicier days or spots like Todos Santos. (If you don't have the *huevos,* don't bring anything over 6'2" and you'll have an excuse to stay on the beach when it gets really big.)

In the end, it's nice to have a quiver of boards available because it's just more fun. So if cost or space is an issue, a good way to pack a quiver is to work it out with your crew so that collectively you will have a nice quiver (to fight over).

Then again, if you're heading to Cabo you don't necessarily need to pack a board at all. The surf shops and camps rent boards (see Appendix). The rental selection has usually been mostly longboards, funboards and trashed boards, but more and more you can find Surftech epoxies of all sizes that are in pretty good shape.

- **Fins** and **hardware**: If you removed the fins to pack your boards in your board bag, don't forget to pack them along with the hardware for securing them (key or screwdriver). Also pack extra screws (for guys like Bobito Sancho, who on one trip managed to lose the fin screw for his longboard center fin and the FCS screw for his shortboard, leaving both boards finless).

- **Clothing**: Consider packing or wearing one respectable-looking outfit (long pants, a "non T-shirt" shirt, shoes, socks), because you never know when you might need it. If you travel to Baja often enough, there is a real chance you could eventually find yourself in front of a judge. Otherwise, you will need a variety of clothes depending on where and when you go. Bring clothes for both hot and somewhat chilly weather, depending on the time of year. Mostly, however, it's shorts and tees. But not white tees. Baja is dirty – dusty at the least, grimy and muddy at worst – so white clothes become brown clothes in short order.

- **Beach towels**: I don't know why beach towels are so easy to forget, but it's not unusual to leave them behind. Perhaps this will help: Beach towels make good board-packing material.

- **Wax**: In Northern Baja, you'll need cool to cold-water wax year-round. Warm-water wax in Northern Baja is about as useful as a tow-board at Doheny. Heck, I can count on one hand the times I have trunked it in the north. Down south is different. For Cabo you'll need cool to warm-water wax, and in the peak of summer pack tropical, too. If you fly in you should bring base coat (which is really tropical anyhow) wax since you should have stripped the wax from your board(s) before packing. Plan for two bars a week, unless you are big on deck patches or you expect to be in Northern Baja or Cabo, as there are surf shops for resupply. And double whatever you are planning to bring to cover your buddy and other waxless "bro's." (The only thing worse than a shoulder-hopper is one of those "hey, bro, got some wax" guys who never, ever, have any wax. Some of these guys do not even have a tan yet and they are bumming wax.) At the end of your trip remember to leave your remaining wax to the locals. Never bring wax home. Pack a wax comb, too.

- **Extra leash** or two: You'll need the second extra leash for your bro who never brings wax. If you're packing a new board, don't forget the leash string for securing the leash to the board. My buddy Bob Towner keeps an extra string tied to the leash plug—a great idea. (Yes, he is the same guy who forgets to bring fin screws. Bobito is awesome!)

- **Ding repair kit**: It used to be that you had to pack resin and epoxy, or Solarez, sandpaper, fiberglass cloth and all sorts of stuff. Now there are convenient ding repair kits with everything you need. Just Surf is a great place to get your kit online (www.JustSurfUSA.com). If you're going to remote spots or plan on being more self-sufficient, bring the big kit—fiberglass cloth, fiberglass roving, razor blade, resin, catalyst, masking tape, 60- and 100-grit sandpaper—for gashes and broken fins. Pick up a copy of *Fiberglass Ding Repair* from WetSand.com or your local surf shop. If you are going straight to Cabo or staying north of Ensenada you don't really need to pack ding repair stuff since there are quite a few surf shops and ding repair joints. Also, if you fly to Natividad they won't want you to weigh down the plane with resin. Besides, they will fix your stick right there on the island. (But you will have to throw the board away or make it a souvenir afterwards as they use boat resin, and lots of it.) If you're flying on a commercial airline, you might get your ding repair kit confiscated from your baggage, as flammable liquids are restricted.

- **Duct tape**: A bit lighter than a ding repair kit. If you are traveling in a pack, have one guy bring tape and another a ding repair kit.

- **Super glue**: To fix your eyeglasses, reattach the rear-view mirror that rattled off, or for needle-and-threadless sutures (see "First aid kit" below).

- (If you rent a car in Cabo) **Soft racks** *and* **bungee cords** *and* **cinch straps** (good ones—you can find them online at www.blocksurf.com and www.justsurfusa.com). If you rent a car you can sometimes rent racks too. If you bring soft racks they may get stolen, and they usually will not handle multiple double-board bags anyway – that's where cinch straps come in. Also, empty board bags don't fit into vehicles well as they are incredibly bulky. So you'll want the bungees and cinch straps.

- **Trunks**: 2-3 pair, depending on the length of your trip.

- **Rashguards**: They don't look cool, but long sleeve rashguards are the call in tropical Baja. They save time getting in the surf (less sunblock lathering time) and money on sunblock. They also help on medical bills - fewer carcinomas.

- **Sunglasses**: 1 cheap pair. You can buy spare or replacement sunglasses for less than $10 from the border to Ensenada, in Camalu and again in Cabo – frankly, anywhere in Mexico. Pack an extra pair of prescription glasses in case you lose one, especially for driving.

- **Hats**: Surf travel requires serious sun protection. Trucker caps are OK, but leave much uncovered. Bring your cool cap for going out, and a dork cap to keep the sun off. Try one of those Australian-looking things that can be crumpled up into your pocket and washed without brim damage. They protect your neck so you will not have Baja lizard neck by the time you are 30. Japanese gardener straw hats are even better. When is the last time you saw a Japanese gardener with lizard neck?

- **Swiss Army knife**: Pack it in your checked luggage if you are flying as airport security won't let you carry it on the plane in your pocket or carry-on bag. That goes for any sharp objects, including fingernail files or scissors. To get the latest, and most comprehensive information on the security rules for air travel check the TSA/Transportation Security Administration web site: www.tsa.gov.

- **Spanish-English dictionary**

- **Flashlight and extra batteries**: There's a lighting shortage most everywhere in the world, or at least that's how it feels relative to the most advanced countries, and in parts of Baja the power sometimes goes out at night. So even if you're not camping, a flashlight will be handy. Headlamps are dorky, but keep you from having to undo your pants with one hand for that 4am piss. Don't forget extra batteries. They can be relatively expensive and they are usually old. Bring extra batteries for your cameras, too. Or just use the flashlight app on your smartphone.

- **Sunblock** lotion: Lots of UV rated 30-plus. Buy the cheap stuff for your body (and the no-wax bro); you'll use gallons of it (unless you use a long sleeve rashguard). Buy the expensive stuff for your face. The cheap stuff stings your eyes more easily, ruining the first half-hour of every session. Look for waterproof, rubproof, sweatproof, UVA and UVB protection. Get sunblock chapstick too.

- **Mosquito repellent**: Generally not needed for Northern Baja, but a good idea for down south in the summer. Deet is the super-power stuff. Its warnings, however, include things like, "Do not use on face...wash treated clothing...avoid contact with plastics...." So it's a bit scary. An unlikely but "healthier" alternative is Avon Skin-So-Soft moisturizing stick. Avon has no warning that you may end up peeling your skin off like a boiled chicken, and it leaves your skin feeling oh-so-soft too! But it doesn't work as well when the Mexican Air Force comes out. There is also Repel's Lemon Eucalyptus, the only organic repellant approved by the CDC. A *Backpacker* magazine test rated its effectiveness at 4 hours. Eucalyptus is a known bug repellent. Long pants and shirtsleeves work great too.

- **Caladryl** and cotton balls: For the nights when you drink too much tequila and forget to use protection (from mosquitoes).

- **Cruex**: (For the guys.) Balls do not take well to days of unwashed wetsuits or trunks in warm, moist, tropical climates. Bring Cruex to prevent or cure jock itch.

- **First aid kit**: Start by buying *Sick Surfers Ask the Surf Docs & Dr. Geoff*, by Drs. Renneker, Starr and Booth. Read the part about cuts. Get cut in the ocean and you stand a fair chance of getting an infection. (Hell, just walking into the ocean in parts of Baja Norte can get you an infection!) The more you surf the more you'll get cut, and you're taking a surf trip to surf more. Remember, this is Mexico; it's not known for its high hygiene standards. Back to the kit… Antibiotics (check with your doctor for a good prescription; tell your doc you are going on a surf trip to Mexico), antiseptic (Betadine is good), Neosporin, a variety of waterproof bandages, gauze, lots of tape, snake bite kit (if you are camping), antibacterial soap, Advil, aspirin (for pain and fever), Pepto-Bismol (for you-know-what), tweezers (to pull out urchin spines and pieces of fiberglass), Q-tips for cleaning cuts and the sand out of your ears, hydrogen peroxide to pour into cuts, scissors, and lots of soap and fresh water for washing out cuts.

If you want to avoid all that work and don't mind paying for someone else to put a great, lightweight first aid kit together for you, look into the Atwater Carey products. Find them online at Wetsand.com.

Unusual for a typical first aid kit, but valuable for a surfer's first aid kit's duct tape. First aid tape is not designed to hold flesh together in the ocean. But if you duct tape over your first aid tape you will have a pretty sturdy package that will allow you to surf even with moderately serious cuts.

Here is one more first aid tip from Scott Valor, a frequent Mexico surf explorer and author of *The Surfer's Guide to Mainland Mexico*: Super Glue. In Scott's words:

"How about Super Glue? Invented by the military to take the place of sewn stitches, it works the same. Simply clean the wound, apply a little to one side and squeeze together to seal. As the wound heals, skin layers with glue exfoliate off. It is a great field dressing and easy to use. I have even seen it for sale down in Michoacán!"

I even read where it was used in the Viet Nam war to "glue the edges of lacerated livers together." Fun stuff.

- **Wetsuits**: Once again, a north/south thing. Down south around the Cabo Corridor and East Cape you'll likely need nothing, but bring a springsuit just in case. Up north and on the West Cape you'll need different wetsuits depending on the season. In the winter and spring, bring something for water in the mid-50s—nothing less than a 3/3 full suit, along with booties and maybe a hood, especially for Todos. Most guys wear fullsuits in the summer, too—2/2s or 3/2s, although a short-sleeve fullsuit's probably best. My buddy Arn always swore by his short-sleeve fullsuit as the perfect summer Baja wetsuit. Also bring along a springsuit (2/1) or shortjohn for the warmer days.

Here is the short version: Spring suit from Scorpion Bay south, many wetsuits from Abreojos north.

- **Wetsuit Repair**: It's bad enough to have to travel with a wetsuit, but it's even worse to have it rip on you when you are hours or days from the nearest surf shop. There are a variety of urethane sealants available, and most surf shops carry at least one brand. The problem is that they really don't work well where most wetsuits rip, which is on the seams. What works best is to use iron-on neoprene repair fabric, such as Aquaseal Iron-Mend. It works great. It's strong and fast; a dry wetsuit can be repaired in under a minute. For extra holding and sealing power use both fabric and sealant. By now you've figured out the real problem: You are screwed without an iron. So pick up a cheap travel iron. Or try a hot muffler. Or bring a back-up wetsuit.

- **Booties**: A good idea for Northern Baja in the winter, a requirement for spring (when the water gets even colder), for lava reef protection, or to protect the tootsies from sea urchin spines. Baja is legendary for sea urchins at rocky breaks. Another good reason to pack booties is as a bandage protector. If you cut your foot you may want to use a booty as a bandage cover and protector (over the duct tape, of course!).

- **Credit cards**: Visa and MasterCard are most widely accepted. (Once you get out of the major cities, however, you will have a hard time finding anyone who takes credit cards.) American Express is often better at solving disputes. I've found erroneous charges months after returning home. If possible, you want to work with a credit card company that gives instant credit when disputing charges, then works on your behalf to resolve the issue.

But you also want to minimize your fees. When you use a credit card outside your home country the issuing bank adds foreign-transaction fees. Those fees used to be small, but have skyrocketed in recent years to where some of the majors charge 3% on any credit card usage. The good news is that some credit card companies give good exchange rates, so depending on the fees you can come out ahead. Check CreditCards.com for comparison charts.

Before leaving home call your credit card companies to let them know you will be using your card outside your home country. Some of them, like Chase, will reject your card when you try to use it out of the country until you call to verify it's you. That is not fun.

- **Cash**: Many of the gas stations and all of the lower-priced eateries and hotels don't take credit cards, and it's incredibly difficult to cash a personal check. (The cops prefer dollars, too, and you will need to be prepared for the *mordida*.)

Travelers checks used to have slightly better acceptance than personal checks, especially in tourist areas, but almost no one takes them anymore. There are ATMs in the bigger cities, but they don't always have money and they charge high fees (but give good exchange rates, and they issue pesos).

If you head south of Ensenada, you will definitely want to get some pesos. American dollars are widely accepted, but less so in the smaller towns and businesses, and they always charge you a premium for the exchange – intentionally or otherwise. Basically, you save money by using the local currency.

If driving into Baja from San Diego, stop for currency exchange in San Ysidro. Once over the border you can exchange at hotels, some other places of business, and *casas de cambio* (exchange houses). The *cambios* charge a small fee for this service, and the hotels give a bad exchange rate.

If you run out of money and need to get some sent from home, ask around for the Western Union *(Dinero en Minutos)*. The fee is high, so use it as a last resort.

- **More cash**: Bring more cash than you think you'll need (but don't tell your "can I borrow some wax, bro?" buddy). Travel has a way of nickel-and-diming you to death. And if the surf is flat you'll want the extra dough for more *cervezas*. It is probably not worth saying, but "more money" means less than $10,000. Any more and you are required to declare it at customs.

- **Calculator**: A $5 Staples calculator for figuring the exchange rate at gas stations and other places where you are easy prey. Or use the one on your mobile phone. Speaking of mobile phones…

- **Mobile phone**: Probably didn't need to add this, as who doesn't always have their phone in their pocket? If your cell phone provider uses GSM, like T-Mobile and Cingular, you can likely use your phone in Baja. Check with your provider first, of course. Coverage is pretty good in Northern Baja from the border through Ensenada, Camalu through El Rosario, and most of the area from La Paz south. Check www.gsmworld.com for coverage maps. Usage rates are high, but extremely high if you don't have a special international plan. Data usage is shockingly expensive, so definitely check with your provider before crossing the boarder for costs and plans, or just switch data off.

- **Address book**: You never know when you may need to call someone back home or send a postcard to your boss or sweetie.

- **Driver's license**: If you plan to drive in Baja, your current driver's license is all you need, unless of course, you decide to move to Baja permanently, which might sound crazy now, but don't judge that idea until you get there.

- **Tee-shirts** to give the kids: Or just shed them along the way to reduce your load while helping the locals out. Many surf travelers I know pack clothes they were about to give to the local charity back home, and then they leave them in hotel rooms and campgrounds as they wear them and travel around. This lightens the load, eliminates the laundry chores upon return, and is a good deed because the Mexicans are predominantly poor.

You don't have to only give away clothes you wear along the way. You can bring your charity box of clothes, toys and otherwise and make your drop-off at one of the town churches. They'll know what to do. And yes, I know this is a customs violation. Read more in the State Department Advisory section below.

- **Surf and skate stickers** to give to the kids: Mexican kids like stickers a lot. (So do their dads.) Stickers are as good as cash (and better than candy) with the kids. Keep them handy for when you need directions or other favors from kids. They also work well to temporarily patch small dings.

- **Cameras**: Maximum allowed is two per person, or you'll have to pay fees. That said, don't volunteer if you have more than two cameras, they never check. Don't forget extra memory media or film, and extra batteries. All are expensive in Mexico, and memory cards can be hard to find at any price. Also know that professional photographers are supposed to have a special permit, so you can get hassled at the border inspection going in if you have high-end equipment or even a tripod.

- **Binoculars**: Saves driving that last half-mile where you destroy the undercarriage of your vehicle. Or the hikes that require you to leave your vehicle unattended.

- **Energy or Snack bars**: And bring lots. Food is not always convenient, there are very few Starbucks, 7-11s or Burger Kings, and preparing meals every time you get hungry is a pain. We usually pack snack bars for a quick dawn patrol breakfast. No cooking or refrigeration required. When you run out you can switch to bananas. Those you can find just about anywhere.

- **Books:** For down time. *In Search of Captain Zero*, of course. And this.

- **Earplugs**: Hopefully, you'll be in the water a lot. An ear infection will ruin the trip. Get Doc's Proplugs (www.proplugs.com).

- **Toilet paper**: This is not Huntington Pier. Restrooms are few and far between, and they're rarely well stocked. Add the likelihood of Montezuma's Revenge and toilet paper quickly moves to the top of the packing list. If you forget TP you can always use your beach towel, or your waxless bro's towel, or maybe corn tortillas. Wet sand works too, or this book…

- **Paper and pencil:** To write down directions, phone numbers, etc. Better still, bring a sketchbook to keep a log and draw your own maps.

- **Watch or alarm clock**: So you do not miss your flight back (Cabo trips), or as the only way you are going to get up for morning surfs after a night of tequila shots. Again, a cell phone does the job nicely. Or you could try that Corona bottle sundial thing.

- **Plastic sandwich and trash bags**: To pack your trash. I know, Baja sometimes looks like one big trash can, but you don't need to add to the problem. Trash bags are also good for wet trunks and wetsuits if you want to get that last surf in before heading home. They also work as raincoats. Use sandwich bags to pack goop—sunscreen, insect repellent, K-Y, whatever your goop-thing is—even if you are driving in, so if any leaks develop you will not stain your bitchin Rusty tank top.

- **Vehicle repair parts**: Once you get past Ensenada vehicle parts stores and repair shops are hard to find. The legendary Green Angels mentioned elsewhere in this book carry some spare parts, but you could be waiting hours for them to discover you, and they may not have the correct parts for your vehicle. Here's a short list. You know your vehicle, so add to this accordingly.

  - Extra spare tire, and make sure you have your changing tools (Extra spare is important for any extended off-road driving. If you get a flat off-road, chances are you will get another, which puts you on three wheels.
  - Tire inflator cans
  - Jumper cables
  - 12-volt air compressor or other tire inflator (For extended off-road driving, especially in sand, you may want to deflate your tires to around 15 PSI. You will need the air compressor to reinflate.)
  - Tire pressure gauge (so you reinflate to the proper pressure)
  - Siphon for gas
  - Gas can
  - Spare belts and hoses
  - Hose clamps
  - Electrical tape
  - Motor oil and other fluids (brake, power steering, transmission, antifreeze)
  - Filters—air, oil, fuel
  - Spare spark plugs
  - WD-40, silicone spray lubricant

- o Tool kit

- o Shovel: To dig your vehicle out when you get stuck. Also for latrine digging. A hatchet can be handy too.

- o Tow Rope, Strap or Chain: For when you are unsuccessful at digging your vehicle out. Get a length of at least 50 feet, and a tow hook helps.

- o Spare vehicle keys: If you lose your keys there you're in trouble.

- o Ice chest: Buy block ice before you cross the border. Block ice lasts longer. And ice bought in Baja is made from Baja water, and you know what that means.

How to Pack Your Boards for Air Travel

Make preparations in advance for your boards. If you start early you'll have time to get a better deal on a surfboard travel bag. And once you have the bag you'll need a bit of time to pack your boards, especially if this is your first time.

Preparation starts with buying the best board bag you can afford. If you buy a good travel bag *and* have padded day bags *and* removable fins, then you are set. If not, you get bubble wrap and tape.

The goal in packing is to make a padded lump out of your board even before you put it in the bag. Tape a towel, old wetsuit or a couple of t-shirts around the nose and tail of your board and make it bulky, or use foam nose and fin blocks. Put the foam blocks on and tape the bubble wrap over it. Bubble-wrap the whole thing. Put the wad into your board bag along with your leash, cinch straps and foam tubing (for securing your bag to the car roof), and your vest or short john, if you are bringing one. It used to be that you would pack everything in your board bag—clothes, towels...everything that would fit and provide extra protection. But the airlines have weight limits now, and sometimes the baggage handlers treat the heavier, bulkier bags worse than others (with anger). So the goal is to get maximum protection with minimum weight. Not too difficult with today's board bags and some extra supplies, especially bubble wrap. Even with all that preparation you should feel lucky if your boards arrive with no dings, as it will happen eventually.

Save the bubble wrap when you arrive at your destination and unpack your boards. You'll need it for the return trip. It's a pain dragging it all around, along with the board bag, but it's worth it.

A word on traveling with surfboards.... All airlines now charge for surfboards as oversized or "unusual" baggage. And they sometimes even check inside your bags, so lying about the number of boards in your bag no longer works as well as it used to. To add insult to injury, they also give you a warning that should the flight be full your boards might not get loaded. (That's where lighter bags come in handy.) It's all at the airline's discretion. And it also means you should be prepared to stay at or near the airport should your boards get bumped.

Another word.... Keep a close eye on your boards, tip porters generously, and you may get to your destination at the same time as your beloveds. Once, on a trip to surf Southwest France (before the crowds) I actually watched helplessly through a window at the Frankfurt, Germany terminal as some goon pulled my brand new swallowtail off the baggage cart and sent it off to Venice, Italy. I learned they were sent to Venice after waiting three days at the Madrid airport. I tried to tell the gate agent what was happening while it was happening...a waste of travel breath. Three days in a hot airport while the surf is going off can feel like a stay in the Turkish prison in *Midnight Express.*

Traveling with surfboards is a hassle akin to paddling out at double overhead La Fonda: Nightmare. Then again, you are on a surf trip, so stay cool and everything will work out.

Airlines

Airline	1-way Board fees	Telephone (from U.S.)	URL/notes
AeroMéxico	$60	800-237-6639	www.aeromexico.com
Alaska Airlines	$20-$75	800-252-7522	www.alaskaair.com 1st board can count as checked baggage with standard fees
American Airlines	$150	800-433-7300	www.aa.com
Continental Airlines	$100+	800-523-3273	www.continental.com
Delta Air Lines	$150	800-221-1212	www.delta-air.com
Frontier	$75	800-432-1359	www.frontierairlines.com
United	$150+	800-864-8331	www.united.com
US Air	$200	800-245-4882	www.usairways.com only accepts shortboards
Virgin America	$50	877-359-8474	www.virginamerica.com only accepts shortboards

Everyone knows there are myriad ways to plan and book air travel, from the "back in the day" method of calling the local travel agency to online discount travel sites to going straight to the source, the airline itself. Getting the best deals on airfare requires that you have time to spare for three things. First, you need time to hunt down your fare, as they change frequently, even within a single day. So the sooner you start hunting the better. Second, you need free time away from obligations to allow for schedule flexibility, i.e., you cannot be too bound to fixed dates. If you can be flexible by even a few days before and after your preferred travel dates you can save hundreds of dollars. Third, you need time to spend on long layovers – not always, but it's often the key to the best fare. Here's a fourth, but it doesn't require time: www.ITAsoftware.com. ITA is the company that developed QPX, the travel search engine that powers the most of the other travel search sites. So you get everything you will find at Kayak, Orbitz, Hotwire, Cheaptickets, Galileo and even most of the airlines themselves, but without the ads and other hassles. And it's faster, simpler and better organized than the others.

When making airline reservations you should always ask for the latest info on surfboard restrictions (e.g., length, weight, number of boards, etc.) as they change frequently. That being said, what the agent tells you on the phone and what really happens when checking in at the airport is sometimes different. Use the prices on the chart above as a guide. Again, be sure to check first.

Airfares to warm destinations are generally higher in the North America winter and around holidays, and lower when the school year starts, but they fluctuate all year round. If you fly midweek it's cheaper than if you fly weekends.

If heading to Cabo (SJD) and the flights are full consider flying into La Paz. While it's further from San José del Cabo or Cabo San Lucas, it's closer to the West Cape, so you can catch a surf on your way to the hotel.

Remember that Mexico charges a departure tax of about $48 that may not be included in the price of your ticket if bought in the U.S. If you buy your ticket in Mexico the tax is included. Either way, be sure to ask if the tax is included.

Locking it all up

Most air travelers like to lock their bags. The only locks that will not be cut of for security screenings are TSA-certified locks. Airport security people have keys to open TSA locks, but supposedly, thieves do not. Who knows? It is better than completely unlocked bags. Find TSA locks online at www.travelsentry.org or www.eBags.com.

Private Planes

Baja is one of the few surf destinations where private planes are an option. That's because there are runways everywhere, although most are dirt. I'm not a pilot, but if you are or have a friend who it head to Baja Bush Pilots (www.bajabushpilots.com) to get the info you need.

Guides and Maps

Surf specific travel maps and guides can be found just about everywhere now, but a starting point is www.surfmaps.com. Since you have this guide, the Surfmaps Baja maps don't really provide more info, actually less, so you're pretty much set. Surfmaps Baja editions come as paper, PDFs or ePubs, and were updated in 2007. If you want to go full on topo, try www.mexicomaps.com. They also carry a variety of road maps, so this is a very good source. Probably the best source for all things printed for Baja is Baja Books and Maps (www.bajabooksandmaps.com). Proprietors Jim and Judy Tolbert are residents and explorers of Baja, so with their knowledge they have compiled what I think is the best collection of Baja books and maps.

The best fold-up-to-pocket-size surf maps and guides are the *Surfer Travel Reports* published by the *Surfer Magazine* (Primedia) folks. They are concise guides to surf destinations focusing on the breaks, and include brief information on how to get there, accommodations, climate, equipment needs, etc. They publish separate issues for Northern and Southern Baja. They are notorious for their errors, but they are cheap, convenient and mostly correct.

A relative newcomer to the surf travel guide world, at least in the Western Hemisphere is Hedonist Surf Company, publishing the *Wave-finder Mexico* surf travel guide. London-based Wave-finder's guidebooks are pocket-sized with great graphics, photos and good firsthand (and secondhand, ahem) info on the breaks. (*The Surfer's Guide to Baja* used to be billed as "the ultimate" surf travel guide for Baja, but Hedonist is now claiming that honor, so I guess we'll have to say "supreme" or "greatest" or use some other superlative now.) Anyhow, *Wave-finder Mexico* covers all of Mexico, Mainland and Baja in one pocket-sized book, so it's a good deal.

Online you will find a hoard of mapping sites, from satellite views to drawn, graphical maps. Microsoft's Bing Maps (www.bing.com/maps) gives great aerial views, especially its Bird's Eye view, but as a map it's lacking the mapping detail that others like Google Earth provide. But the visuals load quickly and the resolution is great. By now everyone knows of Google Earth (http://earth.google.com/) for incredible satellite views, but even Google doesn't yet provide good resolution photos for the remote areas. It's getting there, though. But what Bing lacks in detail Google Earth does a pretty good job of providing. It's not always accurate, but it's pretty good.

This book assumes you have good driving maps. (Different from the surf maps above.) There are some directions given here and there, but to give detailed directions to every spot would require a couple hundred extra pages, and you wouldn't want to pay for those. (This book is already a rip-off!) Besides, it wouldn't be right. Travel Maps & Books makes great road maps. You can find them at bookstores as well as online. Another great map choice is the *Baja Almanac* (www.baja-almanac.com). It used to be separated into California Norte and California Sur editions, but now it's combined into one. Another is the *Baja California Road Map* published by the Automobile Club of Southern California—the "Triple A." If you are an AAA member the maps are free.

Essentially, buy the best map you can find whatever it costs. You will save it in gas money ten times over. And the time you will save will get you more waves. Figure a price for that.

The best travel guide is the *Moon Handbook Baja*. You can find it at any bookstore or at www.moon.com. It has the most detail, good maps, and it even points out surf breaks. They also publish a Cabo guide. Lonely Planet publishes great guidebooks, too – one for Baja and one for Cabo and Los Cabos. Get the Moon and Lonely Planet guides and you will be extremely well covered.

Then there is the real thing: Photographs from space. When you die, if you go to heaven (and all surfers go to heaven, right?), this will be your view of the surf. The most extensive and up-to-date collection of satellite image prints and art pieces are published by SatPrints. (tel. 858-354-6778, www.SatPrints.com). This collection of over 30 prints is the only one I know of and the quality is outstanding. There are prints of individual breaks (e.g., Scorpion Bay, Punta Abreojos, Cabo East Cape) as well as the whole beautiful peninsula. If you can't find your favorite part of Baja, just contact SatPrints and they can usually put something together for you. The prints are priced from $29.95 each, are printed on high-quality, glossy paper, and come from 24" x 36" and up, great for framing. For those that can't get enough of Baja, SatPrints also offers the Baja peninsula in king sized 41" x 96" and 29" x 68.5". I love my prints. I'm looking at Guerrero Negro right now.

Accommodations/Hotels

While Mexico is a beautiful country, it's still a developing country, so don't expect the same standards as you would in the United States, Canada or Europe (Cabo excepted). Then again, the prices are a heck of a lot lower (again, Cabo excepted).

Simply put, the rooms are typically not in the condition you may be used to. The beds are usually too soft and the mattresses too lumpy. The bed sheets usually are not crisp. Room service is rare. Furnishings are often shabby. Don't expect to find a

TV, telephone, free shampoo, towels worth stealing or even a toilet in every room. (Speaking of toilets… The toilets suck. But not enough. Most toilets in Latin America do not flush well and clog regularly. It is often expected and is perfectly acceptable to put your used toilet paper in the trash bin next to the toilet and not *in* the toilet so as not to plug the pipe. So be careful of what and how much you try to flush to avoid flooding your room with used tortillas.) And the rooms can be dirty. Walk barefoot in some hotel rooms and you will feel a sticky floor and end up with visibly dirty feet. And don't expect price to be the indicator of quality and comfort, as there are many discrepancies there.

Given all that, it's a good idea to look before you pay. In developed countries, such as the U.S., most travelers don't check out the rooms before making a decision on a hotel. Experienced international travelers know better. Always ask to look at the room before checking in. You don't want to check in, unpack your vehicle, and drag everything to the room only to find that it's too much of a dump even for a surfer. Besides, often you will find that you can get a better room simply by checking the room first, mumbling a vague complaint to the manager, and then asking if something else is available.

Always try to negotiate the best room and rate. You have nothing to lose. The longer you stay the better deal you will get. One-night stands aren't worth much. Paying cash helps. Here's another trick: If you reserve your hotel room in advance, don't check in as usual. Ask first if they have any rooms and the prices. Often, if they have rooms available, the price quoted at the desk is lower than the price you reserved at over the phone. Check out the room. When you return to the front desk to tell them you will take it, and that you have a reservation, but you prefer the rate just quoted. Underhanded? Well, maybe a bit. But what you are really doing is taking advantage of a fluctuating, supply and demand pricing strategy.

If you definitely do not want to rough it, don't waste your time looking for bargains; just find the higher-priced hotels with the most amenities. This approach will save you time and make your trip more enjoyable. And compared to Tahiti, Fiji, Australia, Hawaii, Biarritz, Maldives, Barbados, etc., you will still be saving a lot of money. In Cabo, travel during the off-season, i.e., the summer, and you will save at most hotels. The waves are bigger, too.

Most of Baja now has Internet access, so you can email most hotels or condos for reservations and other inquiries. Many URLs and email addresses are listed in this guide, and more go online every day. Some hoteliers are better than others at maintaining their web sites, so expect occasional price inaccuracies. So no matter what this or any other guidebook says, always confirm the prices.

As a surfer's guide you will not find hotels here other than those near or within striking distance of the surf. Which is not to say that there is nothing else worth seeing or experiencing in Baja, but you should buy another guide (see Appendix) if you plan on traveling to some of the non-surfing parts of Baja.

Hazards – Be Careful

A reminder that danger lurks in unexpected places when traveling in Third World countries. Especially in Mexico. In the U.S. and other more developed countries there are basic safety standards, typically required by law, that protect us to where we don't think much about potential hazards. This is not the case in Mexico. For an example of how bad things can go, check www.BrentsTravelWarning.com. Obviously, what befell the Midlock family is an exception, rather than the rule, but it's a graphic illustration of the situation.

Driving

As mentioned previously, driving in Baja requires a driver's license or an International Driving Permit as well as the vehicle's registration papers.

Most of your driving will take place on the 1,050-mile long Transpeninsular Highway, also known as the Mexican Federal Highway 1 and 1-D, and La Carretera Transpeninsular Benito Juarez. It's a pretty good road, paved the whole way and fairly well maintained. Nonetheless, it does have sections with potholes, narrow or no shoulders, off-camber turns, and other hazards. Most of it is narrow and two-laned. And much of it is dangerous.

Any experienced Baja traveler will warn you not to drive fast and definitely not to drive at night. Most of the road is narrow and leaves little margin for error. So it's best to plan your itinerary for daylight driving—80% of all accidents in Mexico occur at night. The hazards are many, from the unlit roads with the previously mentioned narrow or non-existent shoulders, to drunken truckers, to the headlight-less peasant family, to the taillight-less 10-miles-per-hour dawdler, to the ever-present livestock. (I have read that cattle are the biggest cause of Baja highway deaths.) Drive at night and something bad will happen; the only question is when.

Most Mexican highway signs show the maximum speed limit (*Maxima*) in kilometers per hour, not miles per hour. But if you see a sign with the English words "Speed Limit," it means miles per hour.

Mexican traffic laws require that when you receive a traffic citation your driver's license will be confiscated until you pay the fine. Since Mexican police officers aren't permitted to keep a driver's license issued in another country, they will ask you to follow them to the nearest police station (jail) where you will pay the fine (ouch) and receive an official receipt (with any luck). This is actually a good option. In fact, if they don't ask you to follow them to the station, you should ask anyway. Much has been said about bribing the police when pulled over. This is called *La Mordida* (the death bite), and for good reason—it's expensive. Going to the station is cheaper. And if you ask to go to the station, good things can happen too....

One night I was out with my buds and had way too many tequila shots at the La Fonda bar. My friends took my Bronco keys and the designated sober-boy Chris drove everyone back to the condo. (It was Chris' first Mex trip, and he was high on the experience. Grizzled old-timers sometimes need a little more.) For some reason I thought I hadn't had enough and wanted to go out some more, but had no takers and had to go it alone. By then I could barely walk, much less drive, but I was Rosarito-bound nonetheless. As I headed into town I drove straight when I should have taken the loop-over right, which meant I was now going the wrong way down a one-way street. I got pulled over instantly. Wasted as I was, I was sure I was headed for jail with a drunk driving charge—not a good thing. The police asked if I had been drinking. I told them I had had a couple of beers and that, yes, I knew I missed the turn and was going the wrong way down the one-way street. Then, without hesitation, I asked to go to the station to pay the fine—quickly—or I could pay it there, it didn't matter to me. The cops discussed it a bit between themselves, so I repeated my request to go to the station. That indicated to them that I knew the ropes and that I probably had nothing to hide, otherwise I would avoid the station. The officer asked if I still wanted to pay the fine there, $40—which I gladly did. Then it was on to Rosarito instead of jail!

(A few editions ago, when I first wrote this little story I plugged in my buddy Arnold as the character. Everyone who knew the real story got a chuckle, except Arn. In later editions I changed it to my other Baja partner-in-crime, Bob "Bobito Sancho" Towner. In reviewing the story for this edition I figured it's time I confessed. There, I feel better.)

Mexico governs with Napoleonic Law, which means you are guilty until proven innocent—a big difference from the U.S. where you are innocent until proven guilty, which also means you have rights. And an automobile accident in Mexico is considered a criminal offense. The Attorney General for the Protection of Tourists in Rosarito Beach is located next to the police station. The phone number for the U.S. Consulate in Tijuana is 011-52-664-622-7400.

If you park your car in town and return to find your license plate missing, don't assume it was stolen. Sometimes, instead of issuing a missing driver (that's you) a parking ticket, the police will take your license plate to the station, so you may find it there.

The legendary Green Angels *(Angeles Verdes)* patrol the paved highways of Mexico with their radio-controlled units to supply assistance for motorists in distress. They can provide a bit of gas, water or oil, and do some repairs if need be. They also have limited first aid. If you break down on the highway, don't leave your vehicle; wait for the Green Angels. If your cell works in Baja call 01-800-990-3900 from 8am to 6pm. (Once you get on the highway look for the "SOS EMERGENCIAS" signs. They have the phone number for help which is probably more accurate.) The Green Angels travel in teams of two, and usually one of them speaks English. That said, there could be occasion for needing the proper Spanish terms for car parts. If you get help from the Green Angels, be sure to tip them well. They charge for parts but not service. If they can't get you back on the road themselves they can call the right people for help. They also can tow for short distances – up to 15 miles.

Conversions

Kilometers	Miles	Liters	Gallons
1	0.62	1	0.26
3	1.86	5	1.32
4	2.48	10	2.64
7	4.34	15	3.97
9	5.58	20	5.28
10	6.20	25	6.60
15	9.30	30	7.92
20	12.40	35	9.24
40	24.80	40	10.58
50	31.00	45	11.88
60	37.20	50	13.20
80	49.60	55	14.52
90	55.80	60	15.84
100	62.00	65	17.17

Get the latest dollar-to-pesos conversion rates at XE online: www.xe.com/ucc.

Sometimes, when driving on long, straight roads outside cities you will come upon slower traffic and the driver ahead may signal you with a left turn blinker indicating that it's clear ahead to pass, at least from what that driver can see. Do not trust that offer completely. Move cautiously and look for yourself. And remember, that left turn signal could also mean the car is really turning left.

Yield to pedestrians everywhere—crosswalks, intersections, even the side of the road. Be extra polite. You are a guest, but you will quickly become an unwanted guest if you are rude. You don't want to become an unwanted guest in another country, especially Mexico.

Gasoline

Time was that gas stations were few, but there are now many, especially north of San Quintín and near Cabo. Between San Quintín and Cabo you should buy gas when you can as the stations are scarcer, most are closed at night and some run out of gas, especially on busy holidays. It's a good idea to carry a five-gallon gas can (full, of course), especially if you are going off-road. A good map will have the gas stations marked, so buy one (see "Guides and Maps"). When you do stop for gas, always check to make sure the pump has been reset to zero before the attendant starts pumping. (There is little self-serve in Mexico.) They will occasionally "forget" to reset the pump and charge you for the previous customer's gas too. That's really annoying considering their pump gauges are not always accurate, often overcharging the customer anyhow. Many gas stations don't take credit cards.

Regular gas is called *nova,* unleaded is *magna sin,* and diesel is called *diesel. "Lleno,"* pronounced "yay-no" is the Spanish word for "full" or "fill-'er-up!" Everyone knows the gas is of low quality in Mexico, so some experienced travelers bring their own gas additives from the U.S. Don't forget to give the attendant a tip, usually a few pesos will do.

RVs

There are many RV parks in Baja, and some offer full hookups. The water, however, is still Mexican water, so fill your tanks where the sign says *Agua Purificado.* The electricity is not always great; voltage often fluctuates and may not power two appliances at once. And you won't find stations for black water dumping.

Most RV drivers don't travel alone, but let's throw this in anyhow: There must be a driver for every vehicle entering Mexico. So if you tow a motorcycle, jeep or some other vehicle, make sure there's a driver for each one or they will not let your extra vehicle(s) in. Well, they will, but there is a bunch of paperwork and fees.

If you don't already own you can rent an RV to take to Baja from Cruise America RV (www.cruiseamerica.com) or El Monte RV (www.elmonterv.com).

Auto Insurance

Mexican auto liability insurance is a requirement, not an option. Your U.S. insurance may give you some limited coverage in Mexico—usually just the border area—but it's not recognized as valid by the Mexican government. So, you need to buy Mexican auto insurance. Insurance booths at the US border are convenient and low priced. When driving in from San Diego, exit from the 5 or 805 freeways at San Ysidro Blvd., before crossing into Tijuana, or off the 5 look for "Camino de la Plaza Exit 1A." You will see a bunch of places to get your insurance. They are all pretty much the same. You can also go to the Auto Club (AAA) before you head down, getting you to Mexico faster on that first day, but it's cheaper at the insurance booths near the border. Or get your insurance on the Internet. One good option, and a quality option, is the Discover Baja Travel Club (www.discoverbaja.com). "Quality" because repair claims are paid at U.S. hourly repair rates, not Mexican rates. This means that, should you decide to return to the U.S. for your repairs, like most do, you'll be reimbursed at U.S. rates. Many policies only pay at Mexican hourly rates, so you will not be fully reimbursed if your repairs are done back home.

You can also try the broker that supplies the Mexican insurance for Discover Baja Travel Club, Adventure Mexican Insurance (www.mexadventure.com). Their insurance automatically includes medical evacuation and plane tickets home coverage for up to four travelers in your group.

Surfrider Foundation members get 10% discounts at online insurance company Baja Bound (www.bajabound.com).

If you are towing anything, it must be on the policy too. Most folks buy it by the day, but you can save money by buying it by the year, assuming you will spend a lot of time surfing Baja.

Make sure you read everything they give you with your insurance policy. It is not quite as simple as here in the U.S. And if you do have a claim, make sure to take care of it in Mexico. If you return to the U.S., your claim may be denied.

Travel Insurance

You might consider a travel insurance policy covering theft, medical, flight delays and cancellations. Know that doctors and hospitals require immediate payment in Mexico. By now most everyone has heard about a guy who died in a Baja hospital because he needed to get to the U.S. for sophisticated medical care, but the Mexican hospital refused to release him until his entire medical bill was paid. Check with your insurance company before paying for travel medical insurance, as you may already be covered. But it's often not the case, or the coverage may not be sufficient, like the ones that exclude "dangerous activities" or an emergency flight home.

Renting Cars

Most U.S. car rental companies will not let you drive their vehicles into Mexico, especially without paying a stiff premium, but you can rent cars *in* Mexico. (The converse is true, too—you can't take cars rented in Mexico into the U.S.) Cars are available in Tijuana, Mexicali, Loreto, La Paz, Cabo San Lucas and San José del Cabo. To rent a car you will need a driver's license, a major credit card, and be over 25 years of age (with a few exceptions). Often, you also need a passport. Rates quoted sometimes don't include insurance, and you need insurance, so ask. When the rate does include insurance, it doesn't include collision and the deductible can be high, so once again, ask. Unfortunately, the selection of good surf vehicles is surprisingly weak, and not surprisingly, expensive, as cars get destroyed in Mexico.

You can reserve a car before you go, find one at the airport when you arrive (a good option if you like haggling), get one in town after you cab in to a hotel, or even rent one in the hotel lobby (nicer hotels). You can often work better deals once you are down there, but also are at risk of not having a car available for you. (The Cabo airport car rental counter is an experience. As you approach the half-dozen or so agents they all start bidding for your business. It makes you feel loved.) You can also get a good deal on a car if you get a package with hotel and airfare.

When you pick up your car inspect it carefully for dents, scratches, a spare tire and a jack. You are responsible for any damage, so make sure you don't get charged for the previous renter's fun or negligence. Also check the fuel guage. You are expected to return the car with a full tank, but sometimes you don't start with a full tank, so check it. You are expected to return the car washed so they can inspect it for scratches, but I don't know anyone who ever does.

While it was previously mentioned that you normally cannot take rental cars into Baja, one company specializes in it: California Baja Rent-A-Car (tel. 888-470-RENT, URL: www.cabaja.com). One-way rentals are available, and they will also rent to people less than 25 years of age, but at least 21 or older.

Camping

By law, all Mexican beaches are public, so technically, you should be able to camp on any beach you like. Unfortunately, it does not really work out that way, but close. You can camp for free on most beaches. But camping on many beaches can be sketchy, especially north of El Rosario, where between thieves with guns and authorities with guns, the odds are that eventually you will meet with misfortune.

Take Pat Weber, for an example of eventuality. After 10 years of Baja trips logging more than 500 days his misfortune came near Quatro Casas. Pat, who is also the owner of the San Diego Surfing Academy, had been leading Baja surf tours for years prior to being robbed at gunpoint while his girlfriend was sexually assaulted in the dirt outside their RV after settling in for the night on the bluffs overlooking the surf. His story isn't unique. His mistake, if any, was camping away from witnesses, but close enough to population to be an easy mark for criminals.

Gunpoint robbery stories like Pat's abound, but nearly every one comes from north of El Rosario. (There's even an account of a pair of *caballeros* who rode up on horseback firing guns in the air and ransacked a truck while the owners were out in the lineup at Camalu helplessly watching the black comedy taking place on the beach.) If you plan to camp in the area from the US border to El Rosario, come in numbers or head to established campgrounds. South of El Rosario you're pretty safe; it's unlikely you will see armed criminals with easy ingress and egress, and frankly, it's just different.

There are tons of campgrounds in Baja costing just a few bucks a night, with facilities and the safety of being on private property with others nearby. Sometimes a campground can simply be the lot behind a small, family run motel or a rancher's land, with permission. There are a few guidebooks dedicated to camping in Baja, with *Traveler's Guide to Camping Mexico's Baja* being one of the more recent updates, and *Baja Camping* a stalwart.

Telephones

Let's start with old-school, landline telephones, as bringing your cell phone can be expensive. Calls within Baja are not expensive, but calling home will be if you don't know what you are doing. There are public pay phones in most towns, but there are still many areas without land-line service. For calling home, assuming you are not from Mexico, look for the Telmex pay phones where you can use phone cards (*tarjetas telefónicas* or *tarjetas Ladatel*). *Tarjetas* are sold at shops and other locations. They are the best deal, easiest to use and come in various denominations. For calling within Baja, use the pay phones; they are cheap.

You can also use call stations—*casitas* or *casitas de teléfono*. You will find them in shops or other places of business. They are basically phones operated by an on-the-spot "operator" who simply dials the call for you for a charge, and you don't need a calling card. It can be a bit more expensive, but not always.

Avoid non-Telmex pay phones advertising that they accept credit cards or collect calls; they are expensive. They are *scams*.

OK, back to the cell phone – check with your provider regarding mobile phone service in Mexico. While you are at it, let them know when you are heading to Mexico, whether or not you sign up for a plan, so they don't block your service in the event you decide to use your phone. Cell calls are expensive, typically over a buck a minute, unless you get an international plan.

Finally, how the hell do you dial those crazy numbers? OK, here goes…

Calling from the US: Whenever calling another country from the US you always start with 011 (instead of 1), followed by the country code – the country code for Mexico is 52. Then you dial the area code (3 digits) and number (seven digits). But mobile phones are a bit different, you have to dial a 1 after the country code and before the area code.

-   US to Mexico land line: 011-52-###-###-####
-   US to Mexico mobile phone: 011-52-1-###-###-####

Calling from Mexico is easier.

-   Mexico to Mexico land line or mobile phone: 01-###-###-####
-   Mexico to US land line or mobile phone: 001-###-###-####

Hotel Rates

Room rates seemingly change as often as the tides, so DON'T EXPECT THESE RATES TO BE PERFECTLY ACCURATE. The following will help categorize the pricing:

"Cheap" = $20 or less per person
"Inexpensive" = A nicer way of saying "cheap," or a little more expensive than cheap
"Moderate" = $20 to $40 per person or so
"Medium" = Something around "moderate"
"Expensive" = More than $40 per person, and probably less than $80 per person
"Muy expensive" = You got caught cheating; you forgot to make reservations; you are really, really tired of driving; you just got your tax refund check; you got your first credit card; you are attending SIMA; you are on your honeymoon; you just plain got tired of dirty sheets; you don't want to get robbed (by a criminal); you are a criminal; you convinced the proprietor that you write surf travel guides and you will give them a great write-up if they comp you for a few nights in their four-star hotel practically guaranteeing years of bookings from upscale traveling surfers accompanied by their Playboy model girlfriends and their girlfriends

Sales Taxes

In Baja they are supposed to charge a value added tax, or IVA, of 15 percent, but that drops to 10 percent in border towns. The Cabo area hotels charge an additional 2 percent. But not all hotels or restaurants charge the tax, especially the lower-priced ones where you pay cash.

Food

Everyone loves Mexican food in the U.S., but those same people are scared to death to eat it in Mexico. I love Mexican food in Mexico too, but I have never gotten sick from eating it. Others, like Bob "Bobito Sancho" Towner get sick *every* time they go to Mexico. At every meal Bob asks me what's safe and what is not. "What about the salsa?" "What about the clam chowder?" I pretty much stick to fish, rice, beans and salsa, washed down with tequila, washed down with beer. My theory is that the tequila kills whatever makes you sick. But that system doesn't work for Bobito. So he starts drinking Peptol-Bismol as soon as we cross the border.

Not that you care, but there are two issues with the food. One: the sanitation standards just are not as high as in the US and many other countries. The second and related issue is that most of us are just not used to their bacteria, and there are bacteria in all food, but these bacteria are foreigners, so your system might not be OK with that. So think before you eat, use common sense, and you will be OK most of the time. You can probably figure out for yourself that dirty restaurants are probably riskier, and cleaner restaurants are probably safer. Busier eateries turn their food over quickly so there is less old food they need to sell. Again common sense, or just follow your gut. (Sorry, had to say it.)

Basic tips: It's safer to eat the well-cooked food (more common sense). So salads, fresh vegetables, fresh salsas and fruit are always suspect. Stay away from cream sauces and dressings served at room temperature, especially those made with eggs. Depending on the strength of your stomach you may want to avoid cheeses. Monday is not the best day to order fish as you could be eating Friday's catch, or worse. You might consider taking Pepto-Bismol, like Bobito does, as a preventative for your first few days up to a week, rather than waiting until you really need it.

If you get the infamous Montezuma's Revenge—diarrhea—from the food or water, make sure to drink plenty of fluids as dehydration is a serious risk. Flat soft drinks are good for rehydration. If the diarrhea persists beyond a couple of days, or includes blood or mucus in the stool, get medical help, as it could be serious, amoebic dysentary or worse.

Enough about getting sick. When surfers travel the real question is, "Where's the most food for the least money?" That's pretty much everywhere, as food is pretty cheap in Mexico.

Tipping

The custom in restaurants is 15 percent of the bill. If you stay in a hotel leave something for the maid, about a dollar a day, depending on the price of the hotel room (some of the upscale hotels add a percentage to your bill to cover all tips). Tip the bellman at the hotel about 50 cents per bag. Tip gas station attendants a few pesos. Tip taxi drivers if they do something special. And, as Scott Valor reminds me, don't forget to tip the Green Angels—*Angeles Verdes*. They are low-paid government employees doing an incredible job.

Water

Don't drink the water. (And if you didn't already know that, well, you probably need more than this book.) What that means is, avoid tap water—don't even brush your teeth with it. Don't wash your food in tap water, and don't drink beverages with ice cubes. Most of the more expensive hotels, condos and restaurants filter their water, so that is typically safe, but it's safer if you don't drink the water at all. Pretend like you are European or from *Ell-ay*.

Emergency Help

Contrary to popular opinion, you can find help when troubles arise in Baja. See Appendix for consulate phone numbers. Other places to telephone for help are:

Red Cross: 066

Highway Assistance: 060

Baja tourist assistance: 078 (business hours only)

Binational Emergency Medical Care Committee hotline: (US) 619-425-5080

What's the Binational Emergency Medical Care Committee? It may be your salvation. For more than two decades, San Diego grandmother and heroine Celia Diaz has headed up the BEMCC, bringing ailing Americans stranded in Mexico back to the U.S. Successfully. If you are in a jam or having a medical emergency call Celia. She has unknotted the notorious border red tape thousands of times using her contacts from Tijuana to Cabo. In a medical emergency, getting across the border in an ambulance can be difficult to impossible. Patients often find themselves dropped off at the border making a 911 call to finish the trip to a US hospital. Celia will help you avoid a situation like that. By the way, Celia's BEMCC is non-profit and operates on a shoestring budget—i.e., donations. Please help if you can.

Immunizations

You are not required to get any shots to enter Mexico, but you should be up to date on your tetanus and diphtheria vaccinations. "Up to date" means a booster every ten years. Hepatitis A is common in the wet season down south, even more so on Mainland Mexico than Baja. There is a relatively new two-part Hepatitis vaccine available that lasts up to 10 years. Depending on where you are headed and for how long you may want to look into it.

Pass the Word

Let family and friends know your travel plans as well as you know them. It may be helpful should bad fortune befall you. Be sure to leave copies of all your important documents (passports, airline tickets, etc.) with someone responsible.

State Department Travel Advisory

The following State Department Travel Advisory has been edited slightly for a Baja focus. (Some of it's redundant as it's been covered earlier in the Background & Tips section, but this is the official scoop.) The actual advisory has more information for Mainland Mexico, especially for Mexico City and places like Chiapas and Cancun. For the full advisory check the Department's web site at http://travel.state.gov/.

STATE DEPARTMENT TRAVEL INFORMATION
Mexico - Consular Information Sheet, November 14, 2011
For updates check the website: http://travel.state.gov/

COUNTRY DESCRIPTION: Mexico is a Spanish-speaking country about three times the size of Texas, consisting of 31 states and one federal district. The capital is Mexico City. Mexico has a rapidly developing economy, ranked by the International Monetary Fund as the fourteenth largest in the world. The climate ranges from tropical to arid, and the terrain consists of coastal lowlands, central high plateaus, deserts and mountains of up to 18,000 feet. Many cities throughout Mexico are popular tourist destinations for U.S. citizens. Travelers should note that location-specific information contained below is not confined solely to those cities, but can reflect conditions throughout Mexico. Although the majority of visitors to Mexico thoroughly enjoy their stay, a small number experience difficulties and serious inconveniences. Please read the State Department's Background Notes on Mexico and the Mexico Travel Warning for additional information.

SMART TRAVELER ENROLLMENT PROGRAM (STEP)/EMBASSY, CONSULATE & CONSULAR AGENCY LOCATIONS: U.S. citizens living or traveling in Mexico are encouraged to sign up for the Smart Traveler Enrollment Program in order to obtain updated information on local travel and security. U.S. citizens without Internet access may sign up directly with the nearest U.S. embassy or consulate. Enrolling is important; it allows the State Department to assist U.S. citizens in an emergency and keep you up to date with important safety and security announcements.

CONSULATE: Tijuana (Baja California Norte and Baja California Sur): Paseo de Las Culturas and Camino al Aeropuerto in Mesa de Otay, telephone (011) (52) (664) 977-2000.

CONSULAR AGENCIES (mainly serving the location city only): Los Cabos: Tiendas de Palmilla, Carretera Transpeninsular Km 27.5 Local B221, San José del Cabo, Baja California Sur, C.P. 23406: Telephone: (624) 143-3566 Fax: (624) 143-6750

ENTRY/EXIT REQUIREMENTS: For the latest entry requirements, visit the National Institute of Migration's website, the Secretary of Tourism's Manual on tourist entry, or contact the Embassy of Mexico at 1911 Pennsylvania Avenue NW, Washington, DC 20006, telephone (202) 736-1600, or any Mexican consulate in the United States. Since March 1, 2010, all U.S. citizens – including children – have been required to present a valid passport or passport card for travel beyond the "border zone" into the interior of Mexico. The "border zone" is generally defined as an area within 20 to 30 kilometers of the border with the U.S., depending on the location. Regardless of the destination in Mexico; however, all U.S. citizens age 16 or older must present a valid U.S. passport book or passport card to re-enter the U.S. by land. A passport book is required to return to the United States via an international flight. All U.S. citizens traveling outside of the United States by air, land or sea (except closed-loop cruises) are required to present a Western Hemisphere Travel Initiative (WHTI) compliant document such as a passport book or a passport card to return to the United States. Travelers with passports that are found to be washed, mutilated or damaged may be refused entry to Mexico and returned to the United States. We strongly encourage all U.S. citizen travelers to apply for a U.S. passport well in advance of anticipated travel. U.S. citizens can visit the Bureau of Consular Affairs website or call 1-877-4USA-PPT (1-877-487-2778) for information on how to apply for their passports. While passport cards and enhanced driver's licenses are sufficient for re-entry into the United States by land or sea, they may not be accepted by the particular country you plan to visit; please be sure to check with your cruise line and countries of destination for any foreign entry requirements. Mexican Immigration regulations allow use of the passport card for entry into Mexico by air, but travelers should be aware that the card may not be used to board international flights in the U.S. or to return to the U.S. from abroad by air. The passport card is available only to U.S. citizens. Further information on the Passport Card can be found on our website.

Legal permanent residents in possession of their I-551 Permanent Resident card may board flights to the United States from Mexico. **HIV/AIDS Restrictions**: The U.S. Department of State is unaware of any HIV/AIDS entry restrictions for visitors to or foreign residents of Mexico. **Minors:** Mexican law requires that any non-Mexican citizen under the age of 18 departing Mexico must carry notarized written permission from any parent or guardian not traveling with the child to or from Mexico. This permission must include the name of the parent, the name of the child, the name of anyone traveling with the child, and the notarized signature(s) of the absent parent(s). The State Department recommends that the permission should include travel dates, destinations, airlines and a brief summary of the circumstances surrounding the travel. The child must be carrying the original letter – not a facsimile or scanned copy – as well as proof of the parent/child relationship (usually a birth certificate or court document) – and an original custody decree, if applicable. Travelers should contact the Mexican Embassy or the nearest Mexican consulate for current information. **Tourist Travel:** U.S. citizens do not require a visa or a tourist card for tourist stays of 72 hours or less within the "border zone". U.S. citizens traveling as tourists beyond the "border zone", or entering Mexico by air, must pay a fee to obtain a tourist card, also known as an FMM, available from Mexican consulates, Mexican border crossing points, Mexican tourism offices, airports within the border zone and most airlines serving Mexico. The fee for the tourist card is generally included in the price of a plane ticket for travelers arriving by air. U.S. citizens fill out the FMM form; Mexican immigration retains the large portion and the traveler is given the small right-hand portion. This FMM is normally white, blue and green in color. It is extremely important to keep this form in a safe location. Mexican immigration agents and federal police have the authority to ask for proof of legal status in Mexico, and on occasion, U.S. citizens without documents have been detained by police. Travelers should always carry a photocopy of their passport data page and FMM. Upon exiting the country at a Mexican Immigration (INM) departure check point, U.S. citizens are required to turn in this form. We are aware of cases where U.S. citizens without their FMM have been required to change their flight (at personal expense), file a police report regarding the missing document, and visit an INM office to pay a fine and obtain a valid exit visa. In other cases, travelers have been able to continue their journey after paying a fine. For more information visit the INM website. **Business Travel:** Upon arrival in Mexico, business travelers must complete and submit a form (Form FMM) authorizing the conduct of business, but not employment, for a 30-day period. Travelers entering Mexico for purposes other than tourism or business, or for stays of longer than 180 days, require a visa and must carry a valid U.S. passport. U.S. citizens planning to work or live in Mexico should apply for the appropriate Mexican visa at the Mexican Embassy in Washington, DC, or at the nearest Mexican consulate in the United States.

Dual Nationality: Mexican law recognizes dual nationality for Mexicans by birth, meaning those born in Mexico or born abroad to Mexican parents. U.S. citizens who are also Mexican nationals are considered by local authorities to be Mexican. Dual nationality status could result in the delay of notification of arrests and other emergencies or hamper U.S. Government efforts to provide consular services. Dual nationals are subject to compulsory military service in Mexico; in addition, dual national males must register for the U.S. Selective Service upon turning 18. For more information, visit the U.S. Selective Service website. Travelers possessing both U.S. and Mexican nationalities must carry with them proof of citizenship of both countries. Under Mexican law, dual nationals entering or departing Mexico must identify themselves as Mexican. Under U.S. law, dual nationals entering the United States must identify themselves as U.S. citizens. **Customs Regulations:** Please refer to our information on customs regulations. U.S. citizens bringing gifts to friends and relatives in Mexico should be prepared to demonstrate to Mexican customs officials the origin and value of the gifts. U.S. citizens entering Mexico by land borders can bring in gifts with a value of up to $75.00 duty-free, except for alcohol and tobacco products. U.S. citizens entering Mexico by air or sea can bring in gifts with a value of up to $300.00 duty-free. **Personal Effects:** Tourists are allowed to bring in their personal effects duty-free. According to customs regulations, in addition to clothing, personal effects may include one camera, one video cassette player, one personal computer, one CD player, 5 DVDs, 20 music CDs or audiocassettes, 12 rolls of unused film, and one cellular phone. Any tourist carrying such items, even if duty-free, should enter the "Merchandise to Declare" lane at the first customs checkpoint. Travelers should be prepared to pay any accessed duty on items in excess of these amounts. Failure to declare personal effects routinely results in the seizure of the goods as contraband, plus the seizure of any vehicle in which the goods are traveling for attempted smuggling. Recovery of the seized vehicle may involve payment of substantial fines and attorney's fees. See also the "Firearms Penalties" section below regarding Mexico's strict laws and penalties regarding import of firearms or ammunition. **Temporary Imports/Exports:** Mexican customs authorities enforce strict regulations concerning temporary importation into or export from Mexico of items such as trucks and autos, trailers, antiquities, medications, medical equipment, business equipment, etc. Prior to traveling, contact the Mexican Embassy or one of the Mexican consulates in the United States for specific information regarding customs requirements. **Property Donations:** U.S. citizens traveling to Mexico with goods intended for donation within Mexico, or traveling through Mexico with goods intended for donation in another country, should be aware of Mexican Customs regulations prohibiting importation of used clothing, textiles, and other used goods into Mexico, even as charitable donations. The importation of all medicines and medical equipment for donation to charity must be approved by Mexican Customs in advance; failure to obtain the proper import permits will result in the confiscation of the medical supplies. Expired medications may not be imported for donation under any circumstances. Individuals or groups wishing to make charitable donations should check with Mexican Customs for the list of prohibited items, and should hire an experienced customs broker in the U.S. to ensure compliance with Mexican law. The charitable individual or group, not the customs broker, will be held responsible for large fines or confiscation of goods if the documentation is incorrect. For further information, visit the website for Mexican Customs (Aduanas).

THREATS TO SAFETY AND SECURITY: Millions of U.S. citizens visit Mexico safely each year. However, crime and violence, much of it fueled by transnational criminal activity, affect many parts of the country, including both urban and rural areas. Visitors should remain alert and be aware of their surroundings at all times, particularly when visiting the border region. In its efforts to combat violence, the Government of Mexico has deployed federal police and military troops to various parts of the country. Government checkpoints, often staffed by military personnel, have been erected in many parts of the country, especially, but not exclusively, in the border area. U.S. citizens are advised to cooperate with personnel at government checkpoints when traveling on Mexican highways. All travelers to Mexico should review the Department of State's Travel Warning for Mexico that provides detailed information about security issues affecting parts of the country.

Stay up to date by:

• Bookmarking our Bureau of Consular Affairs website, which contains the current Travel Warnings and Travel Alerts as well as the Worldwide Caution.
• Following us on Twitter and the Bureau of Consular Affairs page on Facebook as well.
• Downloading our free Smart Traveler iPhone App to have travel information at your fingertips.
• Calling 1-888-407-4747 toll-free within the U.S. and Canada, or by calling a regular toll line, 1-202-501-4444, from other countries.
• Taking time before you travel to improve your personal security. Here are some useful tips for traveling safely abroad.

Demonstrations: The Mexican Constitution prohibits political activities by foreigners; such actions may result in detention and/or deportation. Travelers should avoid political demonstrations and other activities that might be deemed political by the Mexican authorities. Even demonstrations intended to be peaceful can turn confrontational and escalate into violence. Demonstrators in Mexico may block traffic on roads, including major arteries, or take control of toll booths on highways. U.S. citizens are urged to avoid areas of demonstrations, and to exercise caution if in the vicinity of any protests.

CRIME: Crime in Mexico continues to occur at a high rate and can often be violent. Street crime, ranging from pick pocketing to armed robbery, is a serious problem in most major cities. The low rates of apprehension and conviction of criminals contribute to Mexico's high crime rate. The homicide rates in parts of Mexico have risen sharply in recent years, driven largely by violence associated with transnational criminal organizations. Ciudad Juarez and other cities along Mexico's northern border have particularly high murder rates. The Mexican government makes a considerable effort to protect U.S. citizens and other visitors traveling to major tourist destinations. Resort areas and tourist destinations in Mexico generally do not see the levels of violence and crime reported in the border region and in areas along major trafficking routes. Nevertheless, crime and violence are serious problems. While most victims of violence are Mexican citizens associated with criminal activity, the security situation poses serious risks for U.S. citizens as well. U.S. citizen victims of crime in Mexico are encouraged to report incidents to the nearest police headquarters and to the nearest U.S. consular office.

The Government of Mexico has taken significant steps to strengthen its law enforcement capabilities at the federal level, which have begun putting organized criminal networks on the defensive. However, state and local police forces continue to suffer from lack of training and funding, and are a weak deterrent to criminals acting on behalf of organized crime and armed with an impressive array of weapons. In some areas, municipal police forces are widely suspected of colluding with organized crime. Significant administration of justice reforms are being undertaken in certain Mexican states, as well as at the federal level; however, judicial systems are often overworked, under resourced, and inefficient.

Pirated Merchandise: Counterfeit and pirated goods are widely available in Mexico. Their sale is largely controlled by organized crime. Purchase for personal use is not criminalized in Mexico; however, bringing these goods back to the United States may result in forfeitures and/or fines. **Personal Property:** Travelers should always leave valuables and irreplaceable items in a safe place, or avoid bringing them at all. All visitors are encouraged to make use of hotel safes when available, avoid wearing obviously expensive jewelry or designer clothing, and carry only the cash or credit cards that will be needed on each outing. There have been significant numbers of incidents of pick pocketing, purse snatching, and hotel-room theft. Public transportation is a particularly popular place for pickpockets. When renting a vehicle, ensure that advertisements or labels for the rental agency are not prominently displayed on the vehicle. Avoid leaving valuables such as identification, passport, and irreplaceable property in rental vehicles, even when locked. Some travelers have had their passports stolen from their bags within the airport, particularly during peak travel seasons. Remember to secure your passport within a zipper pocket or other safe enclosure so that it cannot be easily removed. Be vigilant of your passport even after passing through security and while waiting in a departure lounge to board your flight.

Business travelers should be aware that theft can occur even in apparently secure locations. Theft of items such as briefcases and laptops occur frequently at Mexico City's Benito Juarez International Airport and at business-class hotels. Passengers arriving at Mexican airports who need to obtain pesos should use the exchange counters or ATMs in the arrival/departure gate area, where access is restricted, rather than changing money after passing through Customs, where they can be observed by criminals. A number of U.S. citizens have been arrested for passing on counterfeit currency they had earlier received in change. If you receive what you believe to be a counterfeit bank note, bring it to the attention of Mexican law enforcement.

Personal Safety: Visitors should be aware of their surroundings at all times, even when in areas generally considered safe. Women traveling alone are especially vulnerable and should exercise caution, particularly at night. Some U.S Citizens who have almost always been unaccompanied and who were walking in isolated locations have reported being raped, robbed of personal property, or abducted and then held while their credit cards were used at various businesses or Automatic Teller Machines (ATMs). U.S. citizens should be very cautious in general when using ATMs in Mexico. If an ATM must be used, it should be accessed only during the business day at large protected facilities (preferably inside commercial establishments, rather than at glass-enclosed, highly visible ATMs on streets). Travelers to remote or isolated hunting or fishing venues should be aware that they may be some distance from ATMs, appropriate medical services, and law enforcement or consular assistance in an emergency. **Kidnapping:** Kidnapping, including the kidnapping of non-Mexicans, continues to occur. So-called express kidnappings, i.e., attempts to get quick cash in exchange for the release of an individual, have occurred in almost all of Mexico's large cities and appear to target not only the wealthy but also the middle class. Review the sections above on personal property and personal safety for common sense actions you can take to reduce the risk of becoming a victim.

A common scam throughout Mexico is 'virtual' kidnapping by telephone, in which the callers typically speak in a distraught voice in a ploy to elicit information about a potential victim and then use this knowledge to demand ransom for the release of the supposed victim. Such calls are often placed by prison inmates using smuggled cellular phones. In the event of such a call, it is important to stay calm, as the vast majority of the calls are hoaxes. Do not reveal any personal information; try to speak with the victim to corroborate his/her identity; and contact the local police as well as the Embassy or nearest consulate. **Credit/Debit Card "Skimming":** Exercise caution when utilizing credit or debit cards in ATM machines or dubious locales. There have been reports of instances in which U.S. citizens in Mexico have had their card numbers "skimmed" and the money in their debit accounts stolen or their credit cards fraudulently charged. ("Skimming" is the theft of credit card information by an employee of a legitimate merchant or bank, manually copying down numbers or using a magnetic stripe reader, or using a camera and skimmer installed in an ATM machine.) In addition to skimming, the risk of physical theft of credit or debit cards also exists. To prevent such theft, the Embassy recommends that travelers keep close track of their personal belongings when out and about and that they only carry what they need. If travelers choose to use credit cards, they should regularly check their account status to ensure its integrity. **Buses and Public Transportation:** Whenever possible, visitors should travel by bus only during daylight hours and only by first-class conveyance. Although there have been several reports of bus hijackings and robberies on toll roads, buses on toll roads have experienced a markedly lower rate of incidents than buses (second- and third-class) that travel the less secure "free" highways.

Taxis: Robberies and assaults on passengers in "libre" taxis (that is, taxis not affiliated with a taxi stand) are frequent and violent in Mexico, with passengers subjected to beating, shooting, and sexual assault. U.S. citizens visiting Mexico should avoid taking any taxi not summoned by telephone or contacted in advance. When in need of a taxi, telephone a radio taxi or "sitio" (regulated taxi stand – pronounced "C-T-O"), and ask the dispatcher for the driver's name and the taxi's license plate number. Ask the hotel concierge or other responsible individual to write down the license plate number of the cab that you entered. Avoid "libre" taxis and the Volkswagen beetle taxis altogether. Although "libre" taxis are more convenient and less expensive, these are not as well regulated, may be unregistered, and are potentially more dangerous. U.S. Embassy employees in Mexico City are prohibited from using "libre" taxis, or any taxis hailed on the street, and are authorized to use only "sitio" taxis.

Passengers arriving at any airport in Mexico should take only authorized airport taxis after pre-paying the fare at one of the special booths inside the airport.

Harassment/Extortion: In some instances, U.S. citizens have become victims of harassment, mistreatment and extortion by alleged Mexican law enforcement and other officials. Mexican authorities have cooperated in investigating such cases, but one must have the officer's name, badge number, and patrol car number to pursue a complaint effectively. Please note this information if you ever have a problem with police or other officials. In addition, tourists should be wary of persons representing themselves as police officers or other officials. When in doubt, ask for identification. Be aware that offering a bribe to a public official to avoid a ticket or other penalty is a crime in Mexico.

One of the latest extortion techniques, known as the "grandparent scam", involves calls placed by persons alleging to be attorneys or U.S. Government employees claiming that a person's relative – nearly always a purported grandchild - has been in a car accident in Mexico and has been arrested/detained. The caller asks for a large sum of money to ensure the subject's release. When the recipient of the call checks on their family member, they discover that the entire story is false. If the alleged detainee cannot be located in the U.S. and the family has reason to believe that the person did, in fact, travel to Mexico, contact the U.S. Embassy or nearest U.S. Consulate for assistance in determining if they have been detained by authorities. Further information on international financial scams is available on our website.

Visitors to resort areas should be beware of possible scams involving inflated prices for tourist-related goods and services and should avoid patronizing restaurants and other service-providers that do not have clearly listed prices. Visitors should check with their hotels for the names of reputable establishments and service providers in the area.

Sexual Assault: Rape and sexual assault continue to be serious problems in resort areas. Many of these incidents occur at night or during the early morning hours, in hotel rooms, or on deserted beaches. Acquaintance rape is a serious problem. Hotel workers, taxi drivers, and security personnel have been implicated in many cases. Women should avoid being alone, particularly in isolated areas and at night. It is imperative that victims file a police report, which should include a rape "kit" exam, against the perpetrator(s) as soon as possible at the nearest police station. There have been several cases where the victim traveled back to the U.S. without filing a police report or submitting to a rape exam, and their attempts to document their case later on do not carry weight with local Mexican authorities.

Some bars and nightclubs, especially in resort cities such as Cancun, Acapulco, Mazatlan, Cabo San Lucas, and Tijuana, can be havens for drug dealers and petty criminals. Interaction with such individuals may put a traveler at risk. There have been instances of contamination or drugging of drinks to gain control over the patron. See the information under "Special Circumstances" below regarding Spring Break in Mexico if you are considering visiting Mexican resort areas during February through April, when thousands of U.S. college students traditionally arrive in those areas. Additional information designed specifically for traveling students is also available on our Students Abroad website. **Transnational Crime in Mexico:** Since 2006, the Mexican government has engaged in an extensive effort to combat transnational criminal organizations (TCOs). Mexican TCOs, meanwhile, have been engaged in a vicious struggle to control trafficking routes and other criminal activity. According to Government of Mexico figures, 34,612 people have been killed in narcotics-related violence since December 2006. The great majority of those killed have been members of TCOs. However, innocent bystanders have been killed in shootouts between TCOs and Mexican law enforcement or between rival TCOs.

Recent violent attacks and persistent security concerns have prompted the U.S. Embassy to urge U.S. citizens to defer unnecessary travel to certain parts of Mexico, and to advise U.S. citizens residing or traveling in those areas to exercise extreme caution. For detailed information on these areas and the threats involved, please refer to the Travel Warning for Mexico.

TCOs have increasingly targeted unsuspecting individuals who cross the border on a regular and predictable basis, traveling between known destinations as a way to transport drugs to the U.S. They affix drugs to the undercarriage of the car while it is parked in Mexico. Once in the U.S., members of the organization will remove the packages while the vehicle is unattended. To avoid being targeted, frequent border crossers should vary their routes and travel times as well as closely monitor their vehicle.

VICTIMS OF CRIME: If you or someone you know becomes the victim of a crime abroad, you should contact the local police and the nearest U.S. embassy or consulate (see the Department of State's list of embassies and consulates). Do not rely on hotel/restaurant/tour company management to make the report for you. We can:

- Replace a stolen passport. The loss or theft abroad of a U.S. passport should be reported immediately to the local police and the nearest U.S. Embassy or consulate.
- Help you find appropriate medical care if you are the victim of violent crimes such as assault or rape.
- Put you in contact with the appropriate police authorities, and if you want us to, we can contact family members or friend.

- Help you understand the local criminal justice process and direct you to local attorneys, although it is important to remember that local authorities are responsible for investigating and prosecuting the crime. Under the best of circumstances, prosecution is very difficult (a fact some assailants appear to exploit knowingly), but no criminal investigation is possible without a formal complaint to Mexican authorities.

The local equivalent to the "911" emergency line in Mexico is "066". Please see our information on Victims of Crime, including possible victim compensation programs in the United States.

CRIMINAL PENALTIES: While in a foreign country, an individual is subject to that country's laws and regulations, which can differ significantly from those in the U.S. and may not afford the protections available to the individual under U.S. law. The trial process in Mexico is different from that in the U.S., and procedures may vary from state to state. Penalties for breaking the law can be more severe than in the United States for similar offenses. Persons violating Mexican laws, even unknowingly, may be expelled, arrested or imprisoned. Penalties for possession, use or trafficking in illegal drugs in Mexico are severe, and convicted offenders can expect long jail sentences and heavy fines. If you break local laws in Mexico, your U.S. passport will not help you avoid arrest or prosecution. It is very important to know what is legal and what is illegal wherever you go. **Sexual Offenses:** Engaging in sexual conduct with children or using or disseminating child pornography in a foreign country is a crime prosecutable in the United States. Soliciting the services of a minor for sexual purposes is illegal in Mexico, and is punishable by imprisonment. The Mexican government has announced an aggressive program to discourage sexual tourism. Police authorities in the state of Baja California recently began enforcement of anti-pedophile legislation. **Arrests and Notifications:** The Mexican government is required by international law to notify the U.S. Embassy or the nearest U.S. consulate promptly when a U.S. citizen is arrested, if the arrestee so requests. In practice, however, depending on where the arrest takes place, this notification can be delayed by months, or may never occur at all, limiting the assistance the U.S. Government can provide. U.S. citizens should promptly identify themselves as such to the arresting officers, and should request that the Embassy or nearest consulate be notified immediately. Also see the "grandparent scam" described above in which a U.S. citizen is alleged to be detained by authorities in Mexico in attempt to get relatives in the U.S. to wire money. Do not wire funds for an alleged detainee until the detention/arrest has been confirmed by the Embassy or consulate.

Prison Facilities: Prison conditions in Mexico can be extremely poor. In many facilities food is insufficient in both quantity and quality, and prisoners must pay for adequate nutrition from their own funds. Many Mexican prisons provide poor medical care, and prisoners with urgent medical conditions may receive only a minimum of attention. U.S. citizens who are incarcerated in Mexico are sometimes forced to pay hundreds and even thousands of dollars in "protection money" to fellow prisoners. Since the beginning of 2002, the deaths of 36 U.S. citizens in Mexican prisons have been reported, including at least seven apparent homicides. **Prisoner Treatment/Interrogations**: Mexico is party to several international anti-torture conventions, and the Mexican Constitution and Mexican law accordingly prohibit torture; however, in its annual report, Mexico's National Commission on Human Rights documents cases of Mexican security forces seeking to obtain information through torture. Convictions for torture or for any alleged abuses by security forces are rare. Some U.S. citizens have reported being beaten, and even raped while in police custody.

Drug Penalties and Prescription Medications: Penalties for drug offenses are strict, and convicted offenders can expect large fines and jail sentences of up to 25 years. The purchase of controlled medications requires a prescription from a licensed Mexican physician. Some Mexican doctors have been arrested for writing prescriptions without due cause. In those instances, U.S. citizens who purchased the medications have been held in jail for months waiting for the Mexican judicial system to make a decision on their case. Marijuana prescriptions (or "medical marijuana") are not valid in Mexico. Individuals in possession of a state medical marijuana license should remember that the license is not valid outside of the borders of that state, and bringing marijuana into Mexico – even if it is accompanied by a prescription – is considered international drug trafficking, a serious federal offense. The Mexican list of controlled medications differs from that of the United States, and Mexican public health laws concerning controlled medications are unclear and often enforced selectively. To determine whether a particular medication is controlled in Mexico or requires a prescription from a Mexican doctor for purchase, please consult the website of the Mexican Federal Commission for Protection against Health Risks (Comisión Federal para la Protección contra Riesgos Sanitarios - COFEPRIS).The U.S. Embassy cautions that possession of any amount of prescription medication brought from the United States, including medications to treat HIV, and psychotropic drugs such as Valium, can result in arrest if Mexican authorities suspect abuse, or if the quantity of the prescription medication exceeds the amount required for several days' use. Individuals are advised to carry a copy of the prescription. If significant quantities of the medication are required, individuals should carry a doctor's letter explaining that the quantity of medication is appropriate for their personal medical use.

Buying Prescription Drugs: Any drug classified as a controlled medicine, including antibiotics, by the government of Mexico cannot be purchased in Mexico without a Mexican prescription. This prescription must be written by a Mexican federally registered physician. Purchasing a controlled medicine without a valid prescription in Mexico is a serious crime for both the purchaser and the seller. Purchasing a controlled medicine with a U.S. prescription is not sufficient and is illegal, regardless of what the Mexican pharmacy may be willing to sell to the purchaser. By law, Mexican pharmacies cannot honor foreign prescriptions. U.S. citizens have been arrested and their medicines confiscated by Mexican authorities when their prescriptions were written by a licensed U.S. physician and filled by a licensed

Mexican pharmacist. There have been cases of U.S. citizens buying prescription drugs in border cities only to be arrested soon after or have money extorted by criminals impersonating police officers. Those arrested are often held for the full 48 hours allowed by Mexican law without charges being filed, then released. During this interval, the detainees are often asked for bribes or are solicited by attorneys who demand large fees to secure their release, which will normally occur without any intercesion as there are insufficient grounds to bring criminal charges against the individuals. In addition, U.S. law enforcement officials believe that as many as 25 percent of the medications available in Mexico are counterfeit and substandard. Such counterfeit medications may be difficult to distinguish from the real medications and could pose serious health risks to consumers. The importation of prescription drugs into the United States can be illegal in certain circumstances. U.S. law generally permits persons to enter the United States with only an immediate supply (i.e., enough for about one month) of a prescription medication. **Criminal Penalties for Possession:** Mexico has new laws that have been touted by the press as making the possession of drugs for personal use legal. Many of the allowable amounts are much less than what has been reported by the news media. Additionally, the new drug laws include stiffer penalties for many drug offenses, and the sale and distribution of drugs continues to be illegal in Mexico. U.S. citizens traveling to Mexico should review this information to avoid possible prosecution under Mexican law. **Importing Medicines into Mexico:** Medications for personal use are not subject to duty when hand-carried into Mexico. Individuals are advised to carry a copy of their prescriptions in the event they are asked to prove that the medicines are for personal use. To ship (import) prescription medication into Mexico for personal use, a foreigner must obtain a permit from the Mexican Health Department prior to importing the medicine into Mexico. For a fee, a customs broker can process the permit before the Mexican authorities on behalf of an individual. If using the services of a customs broker, it is advisable to agree upon the fees before telling the broker to proceed. Current listings of local customs brokers (agencias aduanales) are available in the Mexico City yellow pages. **Firearms Penalties:** Illegal firearms trafficking from the United States into Mexico is a major problem. The Department of State warns non-official U.S. citizens against taking any type of firearm or ammunition into Mexico. Entering Mexico with a firearm, certain types of knives, or even a single round of ammunition is illegal, even if the weapon or ammunition is taken into Mexico unintentionally. The Mexican government strictly enforces laws restricting the entry of firearms and ammunition along all land borders and at airports and seaports, and routinely x-rays all incoming luggage. U.S. citizens entering Mexico with a weapon or ammunition (including a small number of bullets), even accidentally, generally are detained for at least a few days, and violations by U.S. citizens have resulted in arrests, convictions, and long prison sentences. Travelers are strongly advised to thoroughly inspect all belongings prior to travel to Mexico to avoid the accidental import of ammunition or firearms. For more information visit the websites for the Mexican Secretary of Defense and Mexican Customs. Vessels entering Mexican waters with firearms or ammunition on board must have a permit previously issued by the Mexican Embassy or a Mexican consulate. Mariners do not avoid prosecution by declaring their weapons at the port of entry. Before traveling, mariners who have obtained a Mexican firearm permit should contact Mexican port officials to receive guidance on the specific procedures used to report and secure weapons and ammunition.

SPECIAL CIRCUMSTANCES: Weather conditions in Mexico vary as they do in various parts of the United States. From June to November, the country may experience strong winds and rains as a result of hurricanes in the Gulf of Mexico or along the Pacific Coast. Some areas may experience earth tremors. It is prudent to leave a detailed itinerary, including local contact information and expected time and date of return, with a friend or family member, as well as sign up for the Smart Traveler Enrollment Program. **Water Sports:** Visitors to Mexico, including to local resort areas, should carefully assess the potential risk of recreational activities. Recreational facilities such as pools may not meet U.S. safety or sanitation standards. Swimming pool drain systems may not comply with U.S. safety standards and swimmers should exercise caution. Several U.S. citizens have died in hotel pools in recent years. Do not swim in pools or at beaches without lifeguards. Parents should watch minor children closely when they are in or around water. U.S. citizens have drowned or disappeared at both remote and popular beaches along the Mexican coasts. Warning flags on beaches should be taken seriously. If black flags are up, do not enter the water. Beaches on the Pacific side of the Baja California peninsula at Cabo San Lucas can be dangerous due to rip tides and rogue waves; hazardous beaches in this area are clearly marked in English and Spanish. It is noteworthy that even people simply walking along the beaches have been washed into the ocean by rogue waves. Encounters with sharks have occurred all along Mexico's long coastline, particularly in the Gulf of Mexico near Veracruz and Cancun and along the Pacific Ocean coast including near Ixtapa. Surfers and other water sports enthusiasts should always inquire about local conditions before going into the water. Do not swim alone in isolated beach areas. Beaches may not be well-marked, and strong currents could lead to dangerous conditions for even the most experienced swimmers. Do not dive into unknown bodies of water, because hidden rocks or shallow depths can cause serious injury or death.

Rented sports and aquatic equipment may not meet U.S. safety standards or be covered by any accident insurance. Scuba diving equipment may be substandard or defective due to frequent use. Inexperienced scuba divers in particular should beware of dive shops that promise to "certify" you after only a few hours' instruction. Parasailing has killed U.S. citizen tourists who were dragged through palm trees or were slammed into hotel walls. U.S. citizen tourists have also been killed in jet-ski accidents, especially in group outings when inexperienced guides allowed clients to follow each other too closely. Accidents involving breaking zip-lines have also occurred.

Boats used for excursions may not carry adequate life jackets, radios, or tools to make repairs in the event of engine failure and may not be covered by accident insurance. Mariners preparing to depart from a Mexican harbor should visit the harbormaster and leave a detailed trip plan, including intended destination and crew and passenger information. **Resort Areas and Spring Break:** Over 3 million U.S.

citizens travel to Cancun and other Mexican beach resorts each year, including as many as 120,000 during "spring break" season, which normally begins in mid-February and runs about two months. Excessive alcohol consumption, especially by U.S. citizens under the legal U.S. drinking age, is a significant problem. The legal drinking age in Mexico is 18, but it is not uniformly enforced. Alcohol is implicated in the majority of arrests, violent crimes, accidents and deaths suffered by U.S. citizen tourists.

Alien Smuggling: Mexican authorities may prosecute anyone arrested for smuggling aliens into or out of Mexico in addition to any charges they may face in the other country involved, including the United States.

MEDICAL FACILITIES AND HEALTH INFORMATION: Adequate medical care can be found in major cities. Care in more remote areas is limited. Standards of medical training, patient care and business practices vary greatly among medical facilities in beach resorts throughout Mexico. In recent years, some U.S. citizens have complained that certain health-care facilities in beach resorts have taken advantage of them by overcharging or providing unnecessary medical care. A significant number of complaints have been lodged against some of the private hospitals in the Cabo San Lucas area, including complaints about price gouging and various unlawful and/or unethical pricing schemes and collection measures. Additionally, U.S. citizens should be aware that many Mexican facilities require payment 'up front' prior to performing a procedure. Hospitals in Mexico do not accept U.S. domestic health insurance or Medicare/Medicaid and will expect payment via cash, credit, debit card or bank transfer. Elective medical procedures may be less expensive than in the United States, but providers may not adhere to U.S. standards. Additionally, visitors are cautioned that facilities may lack access to sufficient emergency support. The U.S. Embassy encourages visitors to obtain as much information about the facility and the medical personnel as possible when considering surgical or other procedures, and when possible patients should travel with a family member or another responsible party.

The U.S. consulates and consular agencies also maintain lists of reputable doctors and medical facilities that are available to assist U.S. citizens in need of medical care. Before beginning international travel, U.S. citizens may wish to obtain emergency medical evacuation insurance, check with their health care providers to see of the cost of medical treatment outside the U.S. is covered and inquire about the reimbursement process. **Water Quality:** In many areas in Mexico, tap water is unsafe and should be avoided. Bottled water and beverages are safe, although, visitors should be aware that many restaurants and hotels serve tap water unless bottled water is requested. Ice may also come from tap water and should be avoided. Visitors should exercise caution when buying food or beverages from street vendors. **Other Health Issues:** Information on vaccinations and other health precautions, such as safe food and water precautions and insect bite protection, may be obtained from the Centers for Disease Control and Prevention's hotline for international travelers at 1-877-FYI-TRIP (1-877-394-8747) or via the CDC's website. For information about outbreaks of infectious diseases abroad consult the World Health Organization's (WHO) website. Further health information for travelers is available from the WHO.

MEDICAL INSURANCE: The Department of State strongly urges U.S. citizens to consult with their medical insurance company prior to traveling abroad to confirm whether their policy applies overseas and whether it will cover emergency expenses such as a medical evacuation. Please see our information on medical insurance overseas. The Social Security Medicare Program does not provide coverage for hospital or medical costs outside the United States.

TRAFFIC SAFETY AND ROAD CONDITIONS: Continued concerns regarding criminal activity on highways along the Mexican border (which includes placement of illegal checkpoints and the murder of persons who did not stop and/or surrender their vehicles) have prompted the U.S. Mission in Mexico to impose certain restrictions on U.S. government employees transiting the area. Effective July 15, 2010, Mission employees and their families may not travel by vehicle across the U.S.-Mexico border to or from any post in the interior of Mexico. This policy also applies to employees and their families transiting Mexico to and from Central American posts. This policy does not apply to employees and their family members assigned to border posts (Tijuana, Nogales, Ciudad Juarez, Nuevo Laredo, and Matamoros), although they may not drive to interior posts as outlined above. Travel is permitted between Hermosillo and Nogales, but not permitted from Hermosillo to any other interior posts. While in a foreign country, U.S. citizens may encounter road conditions that differ significantly from those in the United States. The information below concerning Mexico is provided for general reference only, and may not be totally accurate in a particular location or circumstance. Public transportation vehicles, specifically taxis and city buses, often do not comply with traffic regulations, including observing speed limits and stopping at red lights. **Driving and Vehicle Regulations:** U.S. driver's licenses are valid in Mexico. Mexican law requires that only owners drive their vehicles, or that the owner be inside the vehicle. If not, the vehicle may be seized by Mexican customs and will not be returned under any circumstances. The Government of Mexico strictly regulates the entry of vehicles into Mexico. Traffic laws in Mexico are sporadically enforced and therefore often ignored by drivers, creating dangerous conditions for drivers and pedestrians. Driving under the influence of alcohol is illegal in all parts of Mexico. Using a mobile device (such as a cell phone) is also prohibited while driving in many parts of Mexico, including Mexico City, and violators may be fined. **Insurance:** Mexican insurance is required for all vehicles, including rental vehicles. Mexican auto insurance is sold in most cities and towns on both sides of the border. U.S. automobile liability insurance is not valid in Mexico, nor is most collision and comprehensive coverage issued by U.S. companies. Motor vehicle insurance is considered invalid in Mexico if the driver is found to be under the influence of alcohol or drugs. **Road Emergencies and Automobile Accidents:** Motor vehicle accidents are a leading cause of death of U.S. citizens in Mexico. Motorists should exercise caution and remain alert on all Mexican roads. If you have an emergency while driving, the equivalent of "911" in Mexico is "066", but this number is not always answered. If you are driving on a toll highway (or "cuota"), or any other major highway, you may contact the Green Angels (Angeles Verdes), a fleet of trucks with bilingual crews. The Green Angels may be reached directly at (01) (55) 5250-8221. If you are unable to call them, pull off to the side of the road and lift the hood of your car; chances are that they will find you. If you are involved in an automobile accident, you may be taken into police custody until it can be determined who is liable and whether you have the ability to pay any penalty. If you do not have Mexican liability insurance, you may be prevented from departing the country even if you require life-saving medical care, and you are almost certain to spend some time in jail until all parties are satisfied that responsibility has been assigned and adequate financial satisfaction received. Drivers may face criminal charges if injuries or damages are serious. **Road Safety:** Avoid driving on Mexican highways at night. Even multi-lane expressways in Mexico often have narrow lanes and steep shoulders. Single-vehicle rollover accidents involving U.S. citizens are common, often resulting in death or serious injury to vehicle occupants. Use extreme caution when approaching towns, driving on curves, and passing large trucks. All vehicle occupants should use seatbelts at all times. Criminal assaults have occurred on highways throughout Mexico; travelers should exercise extreme caution at all times and should use toll ("cuota") roads rather than the less secure "free" ("libre") roads whenever possible. Always keep car doors locked and windows up while driving, whether on the highway or in town. While in heavy traffic, or stopped in traffic, leave enough room between vehicles to maneuver and escape, if necessary. In addition, U.S. citizens should not hitchhike or accept rides from or offer rides to strangers anywhere in Mexico. Please refer to our Road Safety Overseas for more information.

For additional information in English concerning Mexican driver's permits, vehicle inspection, road tax, mandatory insurance, etc., please telephone the Mexican Secretariat of Tourism (SECTUR) at 1-800-44-MEXICO (639-426). Travelers can also consult MexOnline for further information regarding vehicle inspection and importation procedures. For detailed information in Spanish only, visit Mexican Customs' website Importación Temporal de Vehículos ("Temporary Importation of Vehicles"). Travelers are advised to consult with the Mexican Embassy or the nearest Mexican consulate in the United States for additional, detailed information prior to entering Mexico. For travel information for the Baja California peninsula, you can also consult independent websites Travel to Baja or Discover Baja California.

AVIATION SAFETY OVERSIGHT: The U.S. Federal Aviation Administration (FAA) has assessed the government of Mexico's Civil Aviation Authority as being in compliance with International Civil Aviation Organization (ICAO) aviation safety standards for oversight of Mexico's air carrier operations. Further information may be found on the FAA safety assessment page.

MARITIME SAFETY OVERSIGHT: The Mexican maritime industry, including charter fishing and recreational vessels, is subject solely to Mexican safety regulations. Travelers should be aware that equipment and vessels may not meet U.S. safety standards or be covered by any accident insurance.

* * *

This replaces the Country Specific Information dated February 23, 2011 to update the sections on Embassy/Consulate/Agency locations, Entry/Exit Requirements, Crime, Criminal Penalties, Special Circumstances, and Medical Facilities and Health Information, as well as to add the section on Maritime Safety Oversight.

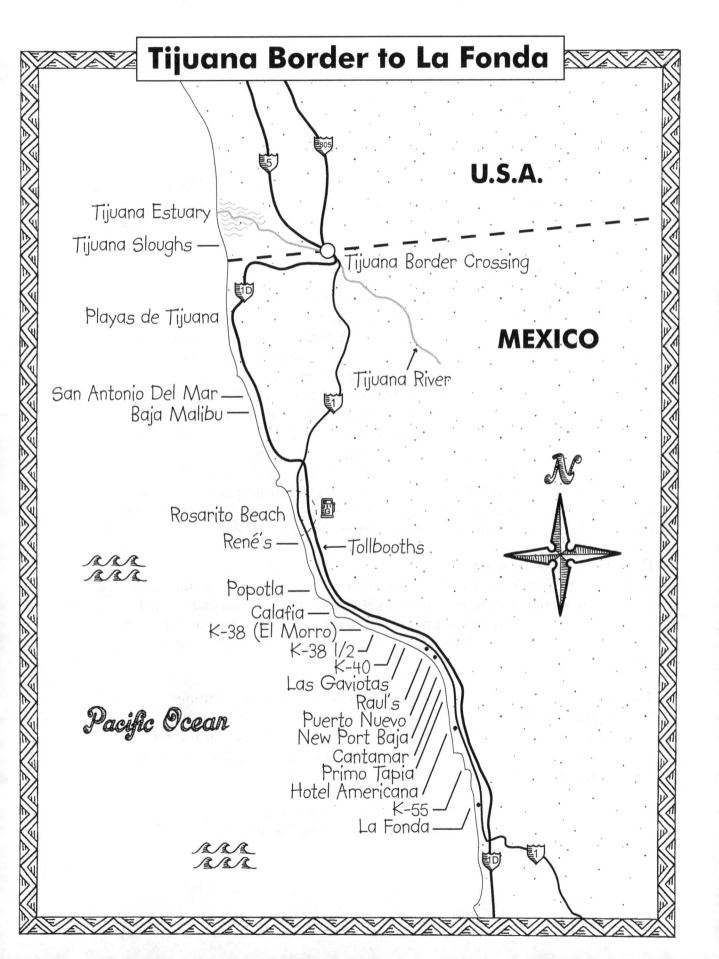

Tijuana Border to La Fonda

U.S.A.

Tijuana Estuary

Tijuana Sloughs

Tijuana Border Crossing

MEXICO

Playas de Tijuana

Tijuana River

San Antonio Del Mar

Baja Malibu

N

Rosarito Beach

René's — ← Tollbooths

Popotla

Calafia

K-38 (El Morro)

K-38 1/2

K-40

Las Gaviotas

Raul's

Pacific Ocean

Puerto Nuevo

New Port Baja

Cantamar

Primo Tapia

Hotel Americana

K-55

La Fonda

TIJUANA TO ENSENADA

There is nothing quite like crossing the border from the U.S. into Tijuana. Your first time will likely be a bit of a shock as you encounter the most dramatic cultural contrast found at any border crossing in the world - straight out of the richest country in the world and into the Third World poverty of Tijuana and the border violence that's barely reported outside Mexico.

While the contrast at the border is great, the area from Tijuana to Ensenada is really a transition zone. It is still crowded (Tijuana itself has a population topping two million, more than the entire remainder of Baja), most everyone speaks some English and takes American dollars, everything you need is fairly convenient, and the main road (toll road) is practically as good as a California freeway. (There are even roadside call boxes installed on the Tijuana-Ensenada toll road. They are marked S.O.S. and are located every two kilometers on alternating sides of the road, so emergency roadside help is no more than one kilometer away.) In the Tijuana to Ensenada area you are likely to stay in hotels or condos; head south and you are more likely camping. Here you will still meet other Gringos and tourists; beyond and let's just say your Spanish improves rapidly. Here the border violence born in 21st Century is real; beyond the peace and quiet of old Baja lives on.

Drama aside, there is a good quantity and variety of surf in this within-one-hour-of-the-U.S. zone. Probably 95 percent of the surf trips to Baja fully take place in the border zone from Tijuana to Ensenada and last less than a week. There are waves year-round, with good exposure to swells from south to north, depending on the break, and a full range of breaks for all levels of experience.

This has always been an easy surf trip. The hardest part was planning lodging reservations in advance, especially in the summer, because with its proximity to the U.S. this part of Baja Norte was always a popular tourism destination. But with the recent violent crime wave, finding a hotel room or condo has become easier.

And frankly, it's probably a good idea to just drive straight through the border area and get as close to Ensenada and beyond as quickly as possible.

And do it in the light of day. Violent crime is so prevalent that it just makes sense to put this area in your rear-view mirror, pronto.

How not to get lost in Tijuana (and quickly get to the surf)

Just after driving through the busiest border crossing on the planet get in the far right lane and look for the "Rosarito/Ensenada 1" sign followed by the "Playas de Tijuana/Rosarito cuota" sign, which is over the turnoff. Watch carefully as the road sign arrows over the lanes don't always line up accurately, which is why most everyone eventually gets lost. You will know you followed the signs correctly when you find yourself on the road with the U.S.-Mexico border fence on your right. If you miss the turnoff you can still recover and find your way to the inland free road that deposits you near Rosarito, but it's difficult for most and a whole lot slower. The good news is you will save a little toll money for the hassle.

Before crossing the border, be sure to check Bordertraffic.com for an idea of how long the lines are.

"*Cuota*" or Toll Road

The quickest and safest way to travel between Tijuana and Ensenada is the *Cuota*, which is the correct term for the toll road. As of this printing the price for each toll stop is about $2.50 (Playas de Tijuana, Rosarito and Ensenada.

Tijuana Sloughs

Legendary hairball rivermouth/delta beachbreak at the mouth of the Tijuana River made infamous in Bank Wright's Surfing California. The conditions at Tijuana Sloughs are…interesting.

It is consistent, picks up every bit of swell, has juice and holds size up to quadruple overhead, especially in the winter when the Sloughs is at its best. It is also polluted and known to be sharky. (But good luck on finding any evidence of a shark attack since 1950.) As with most breaks in the area its shape is best on combo swells, but as a rivermouth there is a good supply of cobblestones to ensure good shape much of the time. In rainier years, sand fills in creating excellent shape.

Excellent shape with minimal crowds? Yes, but it's not easy to surf here. Be forwarned: This is not a learner's spot. You should be a well-experienced surfer and a strong swimmer. In fact, in back in the day, the Tijuana Sloughs was the west coast's premier big wave spot. This was before Mavericks or Todos Santos.

Technically speaking, the Sloughs is really a California break, but it's called "Tijuana" Sloughs and it's listed in The Surf Report's Baja Norte edition. If you want to check it out look for the signs shortly after exiting Tijuana on the 1D and exit at "Playas de Tijuana." Find your way to the beach by heading right toward the bull ring. You can see the break by looking north over the fence, but that's all you can do. If you paddle out and around the fence you bill be making an illegal border crossing. So if you really want to surf the Tijuana Sloughs go back to the border and head to Imperial Beach.

There are four main breaks, depending on the size of the surf, how much you are willing to paddle, and the size of your huevos: Inside Peak, Middle Peak, Outside Peak and Mystic Peak – the latter only breaking on huge swells. And frankly, huge swells is what the Sloughs is all about.

Playas de Tijuana

An easier option than the Sloughs is Playas de Tijuana, which is right there along the strip in front of the bullring. The beachbreak here is fun to good, with something to surf most of the time, but gets some south swell blocked by the islands. Shape is good up to double overhead. The access is easy and the strip there is kind of fun as it's the tourist beach for the Tijuana locals. Never really crowded.

Something to consider, though, is the pollution. All of Tijuana's runoff meets the ocean right here. If you visit the Playas de Tijuana you will need to get back to the toll road in order to head south to the other breaks.

San Antonio del Mar

The exit from the 1D for San Antonio del Mar is just before Km. 22. San Antonio del Mar is one of the oldest Gringo settlements in Baja, and is private now resulting in difficult access to the surf. SAdM holds a mix of surf options. Best known for the beach breaks, there's also some reef to break it up a bit. This is one of those "I remember camping here when there was nothing" places the old lizard-necks (like me) talk about. Now it's a typical Northern Baja armed-guard, gringo vacation/retirement community that's locked out the rest of us, i.e. the surfers. If you can rent condo or "bro" your way in you will find fun to great surf, depending on the conditions. It will not be crowded, and there's nearly always surf here - plus it's less polluted than the Playas de Tijuana to the north.

If you want to get the latest local info broadcast straight out of San Antonio del Mar check Maggie's Madness Blog: marjorieanndrake.blogspot.com.

Where to Stay for San Antonio del Mar

Your best bet is to rent a house or condo. Check VRBO.com. If you rent inside the settlement you can also take advantage of the beachside pool.

Baja Malibu

You can fly halfway around the world for gaping barrels, or drive 30 minutes south of the border to Baja Malibu, the place San Diego surfers go for juicy, winter beachbreak tubes. (By the way, it holds nothing in common with it's US namesake.) Baja Malibu catches swell from any direction, breaking year-round, but gets the best shape from winter west and combo swells at medium to low tide. In the winter the rights are best; in the summer it's the lefts. It is easy to spot right off of the toll road. Take the *"Baja Malibu"* exit and park in the pay parking lot just to the left as you enter the development. Or try looking to the north side of the Baja Malibu housing development for free parking. Baja Malibu is private now like San Antonio del Mar and much of this part of Baja, so the best option is to rent a house or condo if you want to stay for awhile. Despite the name, Baja Malibu is not a mushy point break. When it's small it's fun, like most beachbreak, but with size it heaves, and because it holds its shape it looks easier than it really is. So recent surf school graduates should drive on by or turn around and head up to the real Malibu.

While the surf is good, the crime situation is not. Go online and you will find a bunch of stories about people getting everything from their towels to their trucks ripped off. One guy paid to park and had his car stolen right out from under the guard's nose.

Playa Santa Monica or Villalepro

A bit south of Baja Malibu at the Baja del Mar exit's another beach community—quickly going private—with good rock reef/beachbreaks called Playa Santa Monica. Catches lots of swell, but is best on west/northwests. South swells get good lefts with the right conditions.

Actually, locating surf spots by name in this area is pretty difficult, and maybe not even worth the trouble. It's good enough to know there is a bunch of fun breaks along this whole strip from Baja Malibu to and through Rosarito—including **Rancho del Mar** and **Marisol.** They are mostly beach breaks with some invisible underwater rock reefs to create shape. So head to the beach and look for a peak. It probably has a name, but who cares?

Rosarito Beach

Mostly beachbreaks, broken up by a rivermouth, a few reefs and a pier, all stretched over about two to three miles; who knows. Rosarito beach faces west so it catches most swells and you can usually find something to surf (if you want), and given it's length and variety it's pretty easy to avoid the crowds. The beachbreaks are somewhat walled but get shape with combo or steep-angle swells. The south side of the pier is more protected from the prevailing winds than most of the beach, so it stays a bit cleaner. (Well, "clean" is not the best word. The water is pretty bad from the border to here. Check out the sewage treatment plant north of town with obvious runoff.) The shape is sometimes better there too. Breaks best on mid-tide and up to just overhead. Good spot for beginners.

Rosarito is a party town, but you need to behave or you'll find yourself in jail. (If it hasn't already been mentioned, or it'sn't common knowledge, Mexican jails are not pleasant. Roughly three Americans die every year in Mexican prisons.) I have had friends dragged out of the Rosarito Beach Hotel, a pretty nice place, and taken to jail for no apparent reason. Then again, there is much to do (party) and lots of hotels, so it's a pretty easy Baja trip. And it's one of the few places to meet other gringos, find a surf shop (Tony's) or an Internet café (bajachat.com Cyber Café near the Hotel Rosarito). My most positive thoughts of Rosarito are my memories of camping here before there was much of a Rosarito. But we got hassled at gunpoint by the Federales then, too.

Even with all of the police action, crime has been rising. Armed robberies, home break-ins, kidnapping, you name it. Even the police chief was murdered a few years back. His second in command then took off for a "vacation" in Cuba. Compared to what awaits south of Rosarito the turdy beach breaks just aren't worth it, unless surfing in party town is important.

For a city as big as Rosarito you would expect to find a decent surf shop, but you won't. If you head down the road a bit, however, you'll find the Inner Reef Surf Shop, a proper surf shop. Or just gun it to Ensenada.

Just south of Rosarito on the free road a Federale checkpoint. Stop and be very polite. Driving south they look mainly for fresh fruit and vegetables. You are not supposed to bring them over the border with you. Driving north they look for everything else. Do not be surprised if you get pulled over for a search, especially going north.

Where to Stay in Rosarito

Rosarito is a crowded, tourist town where you can park your car and walk to everything—surf, food, hotel—which is a bit of a rarity for Baja. There are many more lodging choices than those listed below, especially the condo rentals you can find on the Internet, but these will get you started. Good guidebooks or web sites like www.rosarito.org will take you much further.

Lodging Name	Rates	A/C, TV	Credit Cards	Facilities	Comments
Brisas del Mar Motel Tel. 866-538-0187 (US), 661-612-2546	Moderate to expensive	A/C, Cable	Yes	Restaurant Bar Pool Jacuzzi	Credit cards. Was clean a few years back, but some rooms are getting run down. That said, it's probably the best bet in town. Friendly staff. Some rooms have hot tubs. Not on the beach, but right across the highway and a short walk to good beach breaks. Protected parking.
Posada Don Luis Hotel Tel. 52-661-612-1166 Blvd. Benito Juarez	Inexpensive	A/C TV	Yes	Pool Jacuzzi Sauna	Clean motel a little out of the way on the north side of town. Good sized rooms. Nice alternative to the big hotels. Decent restaurant adjoining the hotel.
El Portal de Rosarito Motel Tel. 52-661-612-0050	Inexpensive to Medium, and flexible	A/C, TV			Cash only. On the main drag across the street from Tacos Manuel (great eats) Private parking.

Festival Plaza Hotel Tel. 800-411-2987 (US) www.festivalplazahotel.com	Moderate to Expensive	A/C Cable	Yes	Restaurants Bars Dance club Pool Jacuzzi Playground	Party Central/Spring Break HQ. The "other" Mexico experience. Some rooms have hot tubs and private garages. Discounts often available.
La Paloma Resort Tel. 562-491-5203 (US) www.rosaritolapaloma.com	Moderate to expensive	TV	No	Restaurant Pool Security Guards Tennis Billiards Gym	Condo resort south of the Rosarito craziness. Best away-from-parties option. On the beach. Full kitchens, fireplaces – all home comforts.
Los Pelicanos Hotel Tel. 52-661-612-0445 www.lospelicanosrosarito.net	Medium	TV	No	Restaurant Bar Spa	Quiet, compared to downtown. On the beach. Make sure you get an ocean view room and not an "inside" room. Private parking. Nice.
Paraíso Ortiz Motel Tel. 52-661-612-1020	Inexpensive to moderate	No	No	Restaurant Bar Pool Event Facility	Next door to René's Sports Bar and in front of the surf break. Basic rooms, but possibly the best value in Rosarito.
Rosarito Beach Hotel & Spa Tel. 866-ROSARITO (US), 52-661-612-1111 www.rosaritohtl.com	Moderate to Very Expensive	Some A/C, Cable	Yes	Restaurants Bars Pools Tennis Gym Parking Playground	Range of rooms from older and cheaper to newer, beach view, luxury suites. Children under 12 free. Built during the Prohibition (and because of it), it's a piece of local history. At the pier. (They own it, literally.) Packages available.
Motel Villa de Lis Tel. 52-661-612-2320 www.motelvilladelis.com www.wix.com/motelvilladelis/motel-villa-de-lis	Medium	Cable TV	No		Off the beach with upstairs ocean views. Basic rooms. Cheaper in winter. Great deal for ocean views.

René's

It is always more festive when a surf spot is named after a bar or a restaurant. That's a good enough reason to check out this hollow, overlooked beachbreak in my book. (Hey, this is my book!) Good, consistent surf spot, similar to much of the area to the north, but less crowded and holds better shape on bigger swells. Best on mid and lower tides. René's is south of the Rosarito Pier by its namesake sports bar and RV park (with all hookups). If you're just in for a day trip (not staying in a hotel or the RV park) you can park in the bar's parking lot if you're a customer. Check in first with the René's folks.

Popotla

Heading south out of Rosarito always holds surprises for regular Baja visitors as every year it gets even more developed. The highway has grown from two-lanes with typical Baja pottery shops and roadside stands to what feels like a superhighway with all sorts of new businesses sprouting up daily.

About four miles south of Rosarito at Km 33/34 is a cove with a couple of reefbreaks talked about a lot but not surfed much. Until a big swell arrives. The small crowds are probably due to the difficult access, lack of parking, and rocks. Easiest access is through the private trailer park community on the south end of the cove, but you need to be a resident or you will have to pay to park. You can also get in by parking on the road into the fishing village on the north end of the cove bordering the Fox Studios; it's a longer walk. Even if you don't surf here, the fishing village is worth a visit. You can buy fresh fish at one of the many stands or eat right there, have a beer and watch the surf.

The Popotla wave breaks over a rocky reef on all decent swells, but works best on wests and northwests. Starts working at head high. On good swells a peak rolls in from outside with fun lefts wrapping around the south point, with a short right. Some say it's the best left in Northern Baja. When it gets really big a right breaks on the north side. Local crew demands respect. It's rocky, so it's best at mid-tide plus. Not a beginner spot due to the rocks.

Where to Stay for Popotla

Long time favorite for RV-ers is the Popotla Trailer Park, with water, flush toilets, showers, pool, a great restaurant and electricity hook ups. Even if you don't have an RV, you can often rent a trailer from a "permanent" or do it the old fashioned way—camp (for a fee).

Lodging Name	Rates	A/C, TV	Credit Cards	Facilities	Comments
Popotla Trailer Park Tel. 52-661-612-1501 Email: bajamar_popotla@hotmail.com, popotla@telnor.net	Inexpensive	No	No	Restaurant Bar Pool Basketball	Full RV facilities with BBQs. Some trailers for rent.

Just south of Popotla at Km 34 ½ is the Inner Reef surf shop. It is the best surf shop in the area—the only between Rosarito and Ensenada—and since the original owner, Roger, sold it to shaper Mitch Benton it's now open seven days a week. The beach below Inner Reef, and on the south side of the Popotla Trailer Park is called...

Calafia Beach

Mediocre beach break, but good for beginners, as it's generally small and uncrowded. Stay at the Popotla Trailer Park or Calafia Resort & Villas (tall, white with blue condos – www.calafiacondos.com) on the south side of this beach and walk down to the sandy beach.

Impossibles

Here's one of the few good lefts in Northern Baja, but it doesn't show its form often. Needs a big west or SW. Breaks right in front of the Calafia Resort condominiums; make that right in front of the nasty rocks that are right in front of the Calafia Resort condominiums. Juicy, barreling wave for experienced surfers.

Mushrooms

The Calafia Resort condos were once a monument to the weirdness of Northern Baja development: vacant, slightly tilted, ugly pink, and always "Now Selling." It is now in business for real, so the breaks on either side are getting more exposure and use, like Mushrooms on the south side. Mushrooms is a short, juicy right with a hollow takeoff. It breaks on all swells with decent size, but is best on big souths and southwests and at medium tide. On lower tides it's a problem. Mushrooms is out of sight from the highway, and around the corner to the north from the more popular Calafia (break, not condos), so it's not as well known or crowded. If you are not staying at either the condos or Hotel Calafia, find the gate and pay the Mexicans there to park. Beware if you park on the road; this area is notorious for thievery. Usually they take the whole car. Or you can buy a condo and get secure parking and your own little righthander.

Calafia Point

Calafia was a fictional warrior queen who ruled a kingdom of Black women living on the mythical island of California. Substitute black rocks for Queen Calafia's subjects and you have Calafia Point.

Here's another break that everyone knows but most rarely or never actually surf. Basically, it's not as crowded as its reputation would suggest. This rocky right point needs a strong south—a true south, not a southwest—to really get good, but is ridable on most swells of size. And it gets really good. The wave starts out fast then gets mushier toward the inside. Check it out from its namesake hotel and restaurant or from the turnout just to the south at the little abandoned, red-brick house. (Sometimes you will need to pay to park here.) The turnout is also a parking option. Best at high tide. Sketchy at low tide due to the sharp rocks. At the south end of the cove is Calafia South—also called a whole bunch of other things—with easier access and peaky rights and lefts. Calafia is found south of Rosarito on the free road at Km 35.5. You can't miss the hotel entrance when heading south.

This whole area from Calafia south to Puerto Nuevo faces south, so south swells are biggest and north winds blow off to sideshore. So this is a good spot to check when places like La Fonda are blown out from the north, as it will be side or even offshore. (Same for El Morro.)

Where to Stay for Calafia

The Hotel Calafia is one bizarre place, but a must-see. Big restaurant and club hangs over the surf. Watch where you put your hands when you lean over the rails to check out the surf, there is bird shit everywhere. The hotel features quaint rooms sitting on a beautiful bluff right over the break. Good restaurant and a sometimes crazy bar. If you are ready to tie the knot, Calafia has a chapel and provides complete wedding packages.

Lodging Name	Rates	A/C, TV	Credit Cards	Facilities	Comments
Hotel Calafia Tel. (619) 739-4343 (US), 52-661-614-9815 www.hotel-calafia.com	Moderate to expensive		Yes	Restaurants Bars Nightclub Gift shop Parking	Right over its namesake break. Reserve ahead if you really want to stay here, but the rooms are really pretty crummy for the price.
Calafia Resort & Villas Condos Tel. 866-CALAFIA (US), 52-661-613-2332 www.calafiacondos.com	Moderate to Expensive	All	Yes	Pool Jacuzzi Parking Tennis	Condo towers just north of the Hotel Calafia with surf right out front.

Urchins/Ricky's/Bus Stop/K-36

Driving south from Calafia look for Ricky's Place and carefully (there is a drop off) pull off the road on the right. Here you will find a few breaks, depending on the season and swell. There is easy beach access, food and parking, so it's not a bad stop along the way. One of the more popular and consistent breaks is the reef break right in front of Ricky's Place, mostly called Urchins. It is primarily a right with good shape breaking over and in front of a rocky outcropping. Breaks best on a west, but takes most swells. Lefts break off of the reefs at the south end of the cove.

El Morro/K-38

Here's one that's talked about *and* surfed. A lot. Whenever it's even almost good it gets crowded. Probably the most crowded spot north of San Miguel. South swells are best, since this area faces due south, but it takes in wests and northwests too. El Morro/K-38 is a series of reefbreaks stretching from the Las Rocas Hotel at the north to the point at K-38-1/2 south of the cobblestone beach. When there is a swell and the tide is medium-to-low, it can get hollow and really good; that's one reason why it gets crowded. It is also crowded because the access is easy, it's easy to check out, there is food and lodging nearby, and everyone knows about it even before they ever go to Baja. Mostly known for the rights, but there are some lefts, too. Beware of sea urchins; it's an urchin farm out there. You will only see them at low tide, but the area directly in front of the rivermouth is carpeted with them. I don't think I have ever seen more urchins anywhere. Recently, I found myself stranded on the reef trying to get in at low tide (no booties). My friend (cover artist known for his surf art) "Bobito Sancho" Towner saved my butt (and tootsies) by bringing my sandals out to me while I was literally on my hands and knees crawling over the urchin farm. Bob's smart enough to wear booties. And yes, the bar tab was all mine that night. Lastly, every good surf spot deserves its own surf shop, so in 2005 the K-38 Surf Shop opened up just north of the Puente El Morro. Good shop with all supplies. (See Appendix)

Where to Stay for K-38/El Morro

If you have some money, stay at Las Rocas Hotel. It is just a short walk north of the breaks, and you can watch the surf from the pool or the poolside bar. It is one of the nicest hotels in Northern Baja, although there is a stench by the cliff that never seems to leave. In the old days you could camp Campo Martha at Km 38 ½, but that's now become Santa Martha, where you might be able to find a small rental house. If you want to be really close to the surf stay at Roberto's Motel. It is right on the beach—or rather the El Morro parking lot—next to the fish taco stand appropriately named Taco Surf and immortalized in the Bob Towner pen and ink drawing. Roberto's is basic and clean, but only one of the rooms can accommodate a group of surfers, unless you want to pile into one bed.

Lodging Name	Rates	A/C, TV	Credit Cards	Facilities	Comments
Las Rocas Hotel Tel. 866-445-8909 (US), 619-734-2321 (US), 661-614-9872, 661-614-9850 www.lasrocas.com	Medium to muy expensive	A/C, Satellite TV	Yes	Restaurant Bars Pool Hot tub Spa Volleyball	Oceanfront overlooking the breaks. Great for non-surfers too. Armed guards protect parking. Phones, microwaves and fireplaces in some rooms. Reserve in advance as it's always booked. Full spa.
Roberto's Motel Tel. 661-614-0403	Inexpensive to Medium	No, No	No	Communal kitchen Laundry Board storage	Closer than Las Rocas to K-38; right on the beach. Next door to the old fish taco stand on the beach.

K-38½

Mushy rights and lefts in front of the exclusive Club Marena condos. K-38½ has a funny history. It was always crowded due to easy access and easy, well-shaped waves. Then the condos were built right in front of the break. They were too exclusive for most surfers, and exclusivity included armed guards, so the crowds dropped. Then surfers bought the condos, and the guards started letting the locals in, and others started paddling in from the El Morro parking lot, so it got crowded again. *Really* crowded. The main wave is a right reef/point setup, which doesn't hold a crowd well at all. There is also a left at the south end of the cove. Both break best at mid tides, and take in swells from all directions, although best on souths. Usually it's very un-special wave, mostly a mushy shoulder putting you in constant cutback mode to the inside where it sometimes lines up. Your reward for making the inside section is a long paddle back out to the reef to rejoin 20 of your best friends.

K-40/Rancho Santini

Or K-39…whatever you want to call it, it's just south of K-38½. Good, outside reefs with rights and lefts. Gets juicy on bigger swells. You can sometimes park on the bluff right over the surf if there's someone around to pay.

Otherwise, it's either walk in from nearby condos – Club Marena to the north, or you may be able to find a home to rent in Rancho Santini to the south – or park on the road and hop the fence to traverse the *privado* lot. Better than K-38½ with no crowds. Watch for urchins.

Las Gaviotas

Found behind the huge, guarded Gringo housing/condo settlement blocking views of the surf, as well as access, this reasonably good series of reefs/point setup is a long-time favorite of families, couples and the kick-back and relax on the patio with a beer crowd. Good to sometimes great rights, some lefts. Usually crowded in the summer with condo renters and owners, but Gaviotas can sometimes handle crowds better than other spots because the waves are long and sectiony and there are a few reefs from which to choose, depending on the swell. Just as much fun on a longboard as on a shortboard and good for all skill levels as takeoffs are easy and it's not particularly hollow, except on big swells and low tides. Faces south, so it catches those swells better, but the big winter wests and northwest swells wrap in nicely and offer a place to surf when it's too big at the west-facing beaches. Best on low to mid tide.

Gaviotas is private, so you can't get in unless you are a resident, renter (check www.las-gaviotas.com), or you paddle in from afar (like Los Pelicanos to the south). For renters it's a good weekend trip, whether for the boys/girls (older boys/girls—there is a 10:00pm curfew on partying), couples or families. Once you get in the condos your stuff is protected by armed guards and perhaps even your fellow Gringos. There is also a sandy beach for everyone to hang and play. Many of the condos have views of the surf; all have ocean views. Not your hard-core Baja surf trip, but an all-around good time.

Raul's

Heading south on the free road from Gaviotas you'll see a sign on the right for Raul's Sports Bar. You can pull in right there and rent a room, or find the gate and pay the friendly family $5 and drive down to the edge of the cliff. Here you will find fun reefbreaks with average to great rights and lefts, especially on big swells—anything from south to WNW—and medium to high tides. It is sort of weak on smaller swells, and closes out on lower tides. Go here when it's big and get great waves to yourself; it's rarely crowded. When there are 25 guys out at K-38, there is still no one out at Raul's. Camp on the low bluff overlooking the surf for $5/night—the only facilities are a couple of outhouses…without walls. You can also rent rooms from the same people who own the beauty salon next to Raul's restaurant for $75. There are on and off ramps to the toll road right there, so you can bypass all of the other stuff and make a beeline to Raul's.

Puerto Nuevo

Puerto Nuevo, AKA Lobster Village, is a ritual part of the Baja Norte experience. Those who regularly travel to Baja spend at least one night stuffing their guts with lobster, rice, beans, tortillas, beer and tequila shots in Lobster Village, usually blind to the surf right under their noses. Check it out in the light of day some time. Park in one of the lots down the hill at the beach and look for the right-breaking reef at the north end of town.

K-44½ (New Port Beach)

There are many spots between Raul's and Dunes that go off on good swells, K-44½ is just one. Look for the field just south of the New Port Hotel, and you will find fun, uncrowded waves. The beach itself is frequented mostly by locals, with few gringos ever around. Breaks on south and southwest swells. Lower tides produce fun lefts. Stay at the New Port Beach hotel just north of the break, or the Grand Baja Resort just north of that. Sometimes there's even surf in front of these hotels, but it's better starting south of the New Port.

Lodging Name	Rates	A/C, TV	Credit Cards	Facilities	Comments
Bobby's Villas y Casitas by the Sea Tel. (949) 340-0092 U.S. www.bobbysbythesea.com	Expensive	Yes TVs	No	Restaurant Bar Pool Jacuzzi	Condo rentals just south of Raul's.
Grand Baja Resort Tel. 877-315-1002 (US), 661-614-1488 www.grandbaja.com	Medium to expensive	No A/C, yes TVs	Yes	Restaurant Bar Pool Jacuzzi Tennis	Some studios with kitchens. Satellite TV.
New Port Beach Hotel Tel. 800-582-1018 (US), 661-614-1188, 661-614-1166 www.newportbeachhotel.com	Expensive to muy expensive	No AC, Yes TVs	Yes	Restaurant Bar Pool Jacuzzi Tennis Volleyball	Family-friendly resort type hotel. Most rooms have ocean views. Phones and safes in rooms. Safe parking. Right next to surf at K44½.
Raul's Surf Inn Tel. 661-614-1378	Medium	No, no	No	Restaurant next door	Basic rooms on the cliff over the surf.

Cantamar

Heading south on the free road you'll cross a bridge over an algae-filled lagoon that empties into the ocean with winter rains. Just to the south is the Cantamar Settlement with a bunch of uncrowded beachbreak. The surf here is best in the winter with west/NW swells and when the sandbars build up from the overflowing lagoon, but for the most part, the surf isn't often good. Never crowded, and most swells get in with something. There's a toll road on/off ramp here, along with a Pemex for gas, stores and restaurants, etc.

Dunes

Just south of Cantamar and Prima Tapia giant sand dunes appear on the beach side out of nowhere. These aren't typical beach sand dunes. These are desert-like dunes, but with uncrowded and mostly mediocre beachbreaks on the other side. If you like quad runners, motocross bikes and camping you will find yourself in good company at Dunes, with everyone tearing it up day and night.

Halfway House/Medio Camino

Look for the restaurant with the same name precisely halfway between Tijuana and Ensenada. It's on a cove with some beachbreaks and rocky reefs. Fun surf and no crowds. "Fun" is relative, though, as the surf is more powerful than it looks in this whole area, so it's easy for beginners to get in trouble. In August of 2008 a 23 year-old surfer drowned here.

K-55

Also called Campo Lopez at one time, although technically, the point at the south end of the beach is the Campo. Back in the day it was one of those well-known Northern Baja spots like K-38 and Baja Malibu. Now that it's been developed and privatized it's been pretty much stricken from the list. K-55 takes most swells and gives lefts and rights. There are a couple of reefs out in front of the rocks at the south end of the sandy beach — in other words, in the middle of the cove. Holds its shape with big swells. And on really big northwests there is a right that breaks off the north point and holds shape to double-overhead plus. Good beachbreak waves in front of the sandy beach area (duh). At the south end of the K-55 cove are reefs with lefts. Go around that reef to its south side and you will find the rights known as K-55 ½, or as mentioned, Campo Lopez. The whole area is pretty much for property owners only, so access is difficult, like the next break to the south, K-55½.

K-55½/Campo Lopez

Right and left breaking point and reefs, but best known for the awesome rights on the south side of this long, rocky outcropping. Check it out from the highway above, but be careful as there is no shoulder and a deadly cliff that snatches cars regularly. Campo Lopez picks up a lot of surf. You can get nice little lined-up rights when most places aren't even rideable. But as mentioned earlier, it's private. The sign at the entrance says, "No surfers. Private property. Tenants only." Even the people who buy property in the new K-55 development will not have beach access there.

Alisitos/Plaza del Mar

Between K-55½ and La Fonda is a bunch of surf. Much of it's typical beachbreak, with Baja juice, with a few offshore reefs creating peaks here and there, and more Baja juice. This marks the end of the south-facing coast, as here it turns to face more southwest, so it gets the powerful winter wests head on—big and juicy. Never, ever crowded.

You can camp or park an RV around here for a few bucks a night, but there are no facilities. Or you stay at Plaza del Mar/the Pyramid Resort condos (www.pyramidresort.com). The Pyramid Resort is a condo complex sitting right over some decent reef and beach breaks, with all the amenities and none of the crowds. It is a nice option to the La Fonda scene just to the south. Your wife/girlfriend/family/boyfriend/husband/non-surfers will thank you for sparing them the K-58 camping experience. Right below the resort you will see good lefts (south swells) and some rights (north swells) tempting you to scale the cliffs, but sober surfers will take the 10-minute walk south down the trail to the sandy beach. You and your friends will surf alone, but if you are a beginner that means without help should you need it. And you might, because this area picks up a lot of swell and is usually bigger than some other options.

La Fonda/K-58/Alisitos

From the toll road take the Alisitos exit. The beach here was always called La Fonda, and still is by most, but with the development of the campgrounds it may well soon be better known as Alisitos or K-58, like the big signs say.

Crowded camping ($7/night; $5 for parking only) with a bit of a party scene. The camping facilities are good, with showers, toilets and a paved walkway down the cliff to the nice, big, sandy beach – one of the few in the area.

When the swell drops head to La Fonda as there is always something to surf. And when the swell's up, head to La Fonda for some serious beachbreak juice rivaling Baja Malibu. This beach has a rivermouth at the north end that brings in sand after the winter rains and builds up some nice sandbars. It catches all swells, with combo swells providing the best shape. Even without combo swells, it's often the best-shaped beachbreak in the area. While the campgrounds on the cliff can get crowded, the lineup is not bad due to how the peaks spread up and down the beach, the juicy waves and the beating that comes with getting caught inside. The paddle out is infamous—friends love to recount their "almost drowned" stories about getting caught inside at big La Fonda. Beginners should think twice about paddling out when it's big and stick to enjoying the playful small days.

La Fonda has its own surf shop, Alisitos K58 Board Shop (www.AlisitosK58.com).

Where to Stay for La Fonda/K-58/Plaza del Mar area

Lodging Name	Rates	A/C, TV	Credit Cards	Facilities	Comments
Del Mar Suites Tel. 949-369-5686 (US), 661-155-0392, 61-550392	Moderate			Bar Pool table	At south end of Alisitos Beach. Full kitchens. Six units face beach. Private patios.
Pyramid Resort Tel. 800-721-2252 (US), 951-736-6032 (US), 646-155-0265 www.pyramidresort.com	Moderate to expensive	No	Cash only	Bar Pool Spa & sauna	Most rooms have fireplaces, ocean views and/or kitchens. Some suites have a jacuzzi. Look for "Plaza del Mar" entrance sign and veer to the left. Right on top of surf.
Hotel La Mision Tel. 562-420-8500 (US), 661-155-0205	Moderate	No	Cash	Restaurant Bar Market	On the beach. Rooms have fireplaces. Great views.
La Fonda Hotel Tel. 646-155-00308 www.lafondamexico.com	Moderate to Expensive	TVs	Credit cards with 6% surcharge	Restaurant Bar Gift shop	Right on top of the surf. Most rooms have a patio and ocean view, kitchen and fireplace. Hoppin' gringo bar on weekends.

Playa La Misión

This is not the beach in front of the Hotel La Misión. This is just south of La Fonda where there is a stretch with limited access and a ton of totally uncrowded surf, mostly beachbreaks. Totally uncrowded and often a nice diversion from La Fonda. You can access the surf by taking a long walk along the beach south from La Fonda, or walking north from the public beach south of the bluff (check the point at the south end of the sandy beach; there are often good lefts), or park on the bluff and hike down. The north end of the area is private, so access is difficult. The south end, which is the beach with signs for La Misión, is a big sandy public beach where the locals hang on weekends. Access is very easy from the toll road, and the surf is fun and consistent here too. *The Surf Report* places La Misión north of La Fonda—probably in front of the hotel with that name.

Your free road beachside travels end just north of the sandy public beach as the road turns inland and doesn't return to the beach until you reach the north end of Ensenada. It's slower, and you can't check the surf, but you will skip a tollbooth. The entrance to the toll road heading south is between Hotel La Mision and La Fonda.

La Salina

The next sandy beach to the south is La Salina. Wikipedia describes La Salina as a "gringo community", but you will see it for what it really is, another stretch of Baja coast with a ton of uncrowded beachbreak. (Yes, Baja has a lot of surf.) La Salina is probably best known for the giant, well-equipped Baja Seasons RV Park, but it's also the first boat marina south of the border (240 slips, up to 100 feet). And there's surf.

Where to Stay Around La Salina

Lodging Name	Rates	A/C, TV	Credit Cards	Facilities	Comments
Baja Seasons Beach Resort Tel. 800-791-6562 (US), 646-155-4015, 6 or 7 (Mex) www.baja-seasons.com	Moderate to expensive	A/C, Cable	Yes	Pool Jacuzzi Laundry Secured parking	Right on the beach. Hotel rooms, villas, RV park and camping. Kitchens. Great for kids, with the pool, ping pong and miniature golf. Great for adults with tennis, horseback riding and golf (a couple of miles away). TVs and
La Salina Beach Hotel www.lasalinabeachhotel.com	Moderate	No	Cash	Restaurant Bar	Spartan rooms with balconies above restaurant and bar. Free wifi.

Harry's

Harry's was a heavy, ledging, hollow right point that broke over a shallow rock reef with urchins galore. It was not a spot for beginners. It was a secret spot until January 2005 when all of the surf magazines and everyone else sounded the alarm that the break was about to be lost to development. (Well, actually it was a secret spot until featured on the cover of the May 2003 *Surfer*, and in the article, "Diamonds and Dust." Harry's was not named, and directions were withheld.) Since then, Sempra/Shell has built a liquefied-natural-gas terminal. In a way, the terminal is a monument to secret spots everywhere. It is easier to develop at a secret spot as there is no one to complain—no closed hotels, restaurants, surf shops or any of the other things that pop up around great surf breaks. To see the before and after go to Google Earth where there are photos from 2004 and 2006. But don't linger, the next stop is the legendary Salsipuedes.

Salsipuedes

Heading south from here you'll experience some of the most spectacular ocean vistas in the world. But the crown jewel of those vistas comes from the inside of a Salsipuedes barrel, should you be so lucky. It starts by simply looking for the big green road sign, pinpointing the spot.

Salsipuedes, which means "leave if you can" is one of Baja's most legendary spots. Most attribute the name to the steep, difficult road leading down to the campgrounds and break. But maybe it's due to the excellent waves. There are two main breaks here. On the north side of the point is a fun reef break with rights and lefts breaking best on northwest swells. Good surf that stays glassy with the kelp beds. On the south side of the point it gets more interesting. Six-foot-plus west to northwest swells wrap around the point for thick, hollow, perfect rights peeling across the south-facing reef/point. Most people have heard of the good waves at Salsipuedes, but what they don't know is that this wave is heavy. No surf schools, Bics or softtops here. Summer souths bring good lefts and some rights arount the point toward the north side. Salsipuedes needs size, whatever the swell direction. The right on the south side doesn't break often. Private campgrounds right in front of the summer break in a grove of olive trees. The cost is about $5 to $10 a day—the same charge for parking even if you don't camp. There are also condos for rent. The road in and out can be extremely difficult to impossible to negotiate after winter rains. Leave, if you can.

Salsipuedes to Punta San José

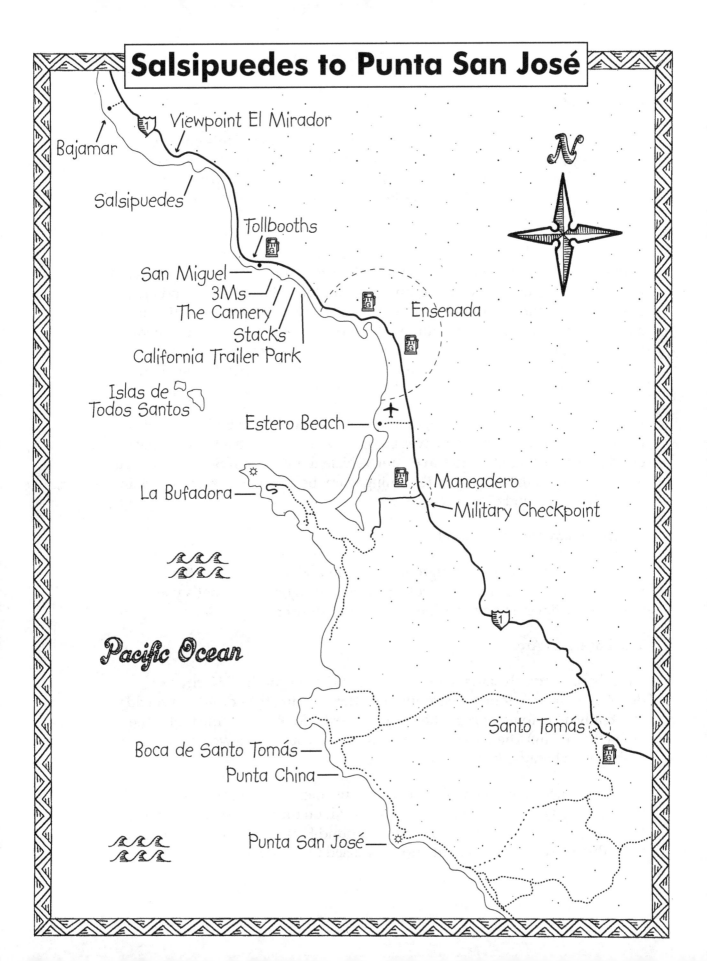

Bajamar

Viewpoint El Mirador

Salsipuedes

Tollbooths

San Miguel

3Ms

The Cannery

Stacks

California Trailer Park

Ensenada

Islas de Todos Santos

Estero Beach

La Bufadora

Maneadero

Military Checkpoint

Pacific Ocean

Santo Tomás

Boca de Santo Tomás

Punta China

Punta San José

San Miguel

Amazingly, San Miguel was left out of a previous edition of this guide book. "Amazingly," because it's possibly the most crowded spot in the entire peninsula. And "amazingly" because it's one of the best right points in the entire peninsula, too. Surfline describes it as "...consistently the best wave in Northern Baja." Sound good?

San Miguel is a classic right cobblestone rivermouth break. ("Cobblestone" may not be the best description, as the rocks are bowling ball size and bigger.) Fast, sometimes hollow with size, and fun, San Miguel faces south and breaks best with wrapping west and northwest swells, low to mid-tide. Getting in and out at low tide is no fun with the slippery boulders and urchins. There is a bigger nightmare, though: Crazy crowds on weekends with gringos, campers from all over the world, and locals. Nonetheless, San Miguel is an awesomely fun wave and holds its shape with size.

It's also awesomely easy to find, as it's right there at the toll both north of Ensenada. In fact, you can pull over before or after paying the toll to check out the surf. Just don't try to leave your vehicle there. To surf San Miguel you will need to pay the toll, if you're coming from the north, then pay to park in the lot/campgrounds.

Where to Stay for San Miguel

The Villa de San Miguel Campground is a good option. You have the restaurant and bar there, so it's not completely roughing it (if that's your issue). They have electricity, water, toilets and showers.

The Ensenada Area

It all changes here. It starts with the hustle and bustle of the first city not devoted entirely to tourism encountered after crossing the border. (Ensenada is actually a big tourist destination, it just doesn't look or feel much like one when driving in.) Then once you pass Ensenada you may as well have driven to the moon because you are now out there.

One of the nice things about Ensenada is convenience, like surf shops. You'll find them as you pull into town from the north on the main road by making a left at Lopez Mateos. They're in the area around Hussong's, Quiksilver and everything else. The Baja Board Shop that used to be just north of town near the Papagayo Hotel has moved into Ensenada, too. And naturally, there are tons of hotels, restaurants, bars and other goodies. And nearby surf, like…

3Ms

Rocky reefbreaks on the north end of a sandy beach less than a kilometer south of the tollbooths. Breaks best on winter swells, from west to NW, and can get really good. More locals than gringos. This whole area between San Miguel and Ensenada, actually called Sauzel, is polluted and sharky due to the fish canneries.

The Cannery

Sandy beach, but rocky, stinky and sharky. Decent reef breaks in front of the fish canneries and processing plants. Those features are a nice shark invite, but this writer has never heard of anyone becoming the main course for one of the men in the grey suits. Florida beaches are way more dangerous. Pretty easy to find. From the north heading south, look for the "Tecate Ruta Vincola" road sign and make a right, but head toward the beach.

Stacks

Just south of the cannery and the jetties is a reef with great lefts and slower rights on northwest swells. I don't know where the stacks went, but pull off into one of the small dirt lots (be careful!) south of the cannery and you'll find it. As with all of Sauzel, Stacks is popular with the locals.

California Trailer Park

AKA Trailer Parks. Reefbreak with rights and lefts in front of the California Hotel R.V. It is probably easier to check out and access from the Ramona Hotel just south of the California RV Park & Motel. The CRVP&M has steps going right to the cobblestone beach in front of the break, or you can stay at the previously mentioned Ramona or the Posada del Mar just to the north. The reef needs some swell to start working, but not that much. Best on west and northwest swells and medium to high tides. Rocky (hence, better on higher tides), so you might want to bring booties, but good shape (A-frame peak with rights longer than lefts) and relatively easy access.

Islas de Todos Santos

World famous, world class, big wave found on the islands 12 miles offshore of Ensenada. Open any surf magazine in the winter and you will be sure to see Todos photos featuring full-suited big-wave hellmen racing the boil at **Killers**. Killers is on the western-most tip of the north island, breaking off an appendix-like point. Breaks in winter on west to northwest swells. Usually at least twice as big as the mainland, Killers can hold surf as big as it gets, but there's also surf on the smaller days. On bigger days it's not for the faint of heart or short of gun. Numerous global biggest-wave-of-the-year surfing awards have been won by surfers at Todos, so there's another clue to how big it can get. If you want to get good information on surfing Killers, look for the *Surfing Magazine* article, "How to Surf Todos Santos" (January 2006) by Mike Parsons. By the way, there is no need to call this Killers, everyone just calls it "Todos" anyhow.

There are a couple other waves on the north island, Chickens and Urchins. Both are good breaks. Urchins is a left that breaks on the other side of the rocks from Killers on the north side of the island. Smaller than Killers, and away from the craziness. Chickens is a right found at the southwest corner of this island.

The south island is home to at least two breaks, **Rarely's** and **Thor's Hammer**. Thor's Hammer is a summer south swell break with lefts and rights, Rarely's a winter break.

You will need a boat to get here which you will hire out of the Ensenada area. Check with Juanito's Boats in the Ensenada harbor at the Malecon (tel. 646-174-0953, www.sailorschoice.com/juanitos). Or head just south of Ensenada and you can go with Mike Bonner and his Ojo del Huracan surf, dive and fishing tours service. Mike offers one-day trips; he can put you up with room and board, and he arranges packages. Mike operates out of the La Jolla Beach Camp (#66G) in Punta Banda (tel. 619-954-9798 in the U.S., or 011-52-646-154-2753; Email Mike at ojodelhuracan@yahoo.com). To find La Jolla Beach Camp, just head toward La Bufadora and follow the signs. You can check around and you will find other fishermen and boat owners who will take you out to the islands. But that's Mike's business, so he is a good bet.

If you have your own boat the nearest boat ramps are (1) just as you come into Ensenada from the north at the Hotel and Marina Coral, (2) at Estero

Beach south of town, and (3) the campgrounds at the base of Punta Banda. To reach #3 take the road marked "La Bufadora" at Maneadero south of Ensenada and look for Campo La Jolla and Campo Villarino. Be careful if this is your first trip out there. Guys have lost their boats.

You can camp on Todos Santos, but most boat in for day trips.

Where to Stay Around Ensenada

Lodging Name	Rates	A/C, TV	Credit Cards	Facilities	Comments
California RV Hotel Tel. 011-52-646-174-6033	Inexpensive	No	No	Restaurant	Motel/RV park with full hook ups. North of Ensenada at Km 103/104 near San Miguel and 3Ms with surf right out front. RV park often full.
Desert Inn (formerly La Pinta Hotels) Tel. 800-542-3283 (US), 800-026-3605 in Mexico www.desertinns.com http://www.lapintahotels.com	Moderate	No, Cable/ Sat	Yes	Restaurant Bar Pool	In town across from the Post Office near the PEMEX on Lopez Mateo. Not a bad option. No parking, but they have a guard to watch guests' cars parked on the street.
Hotel Bahía Tel. 888-308-9048 (US), 800-025-4003 (Mex) www.hotelbahia.com.mx	Moderate to expensive	A/C, Cable	Yes	Restaurant Bar Secured parking Wifi	On the main road in the middle of Ensenada (Costero). Save toll tickets for discounts. Or just ask, it's easy to negotiate. Not a bad choice for the price, but don't walk barefoot in your room; scummy floors.
Hotel Coral and Marina Tel. 800-862-9020 (US), 011-52-646-175-0000 www.hotelcoral.com	Expensive	A/C, Cable	Yes	Restaurant Bar Pool, jacuzzi Boat launch Secured parking Wifi	Full service marina with 24-hour boat launch for Todos and other trips. Lower rates on weekdays. Largest resort in the area. There's pretty much everything you can ask for here.
Hotel El Cid Best Western Tel. 800-ELCID-05 (US), 011-52-646-178-2401, 02, 03 www.hotelelcid.com.mx	Moderate to expensive AAA discount	A/C, Cable	Yes	Restaurant Pool, jacuzzi Secured parking Free Wifi	In-town hotel close to the party but far from the surf. Jacuzzis in suites overlooking the bay. Refrigerators in rooms. Free continental breakfast.
Las Rosas Hotel Tel. 800-5644-0165 (US), 011-52-646-174-4595 www.lasrosas.com	Expensive	A/C, TVs	Yes	Restaurant Bar Pool, jacuzzi Health club Tennis Racquetball Golf	Upscale and luxurious hotel. At the north end of Bahia de Todos Santos overlooking the bay between San Miguel and Ensenada. All rooms have balconies with ocean views. Some Jacuzzis, kitchenettes and fireplaces in rooms.
Hotel Sausalito Tel. 011-52-646-174-6145 www.hotelsausalito.com/mx	Inexpensive	No	No	Restaurant Sports Bar Pool Free Wifi	At Km 102/103 just south of San Miguel and 3Ms in El Sauzel. Frig and microwave in room.

Las Palmas Hotel Tel. 011-52-646-177-1708 www.paraisolaspalmas.com	Moderate	AC, Cable	Yes	Restaurant Bar Pool, Jacuzzi Parking Internet Convention Center	Formerly Paraiso Las Palmas. Secured parking. In the middle of town at the bay on Sangines off of Costero.
Posada del Mar Tel. 011-52 (646) 174-6335 www.ensenadaposadadelmar.com	Moderate	No, no	No		Just north of California Trailer Park reef breaks. Paddle right out to surf. Kitchenettes. Special rates for longer stays.
Punta Morro Hotel Tel. 800-526-6676 (US), 011-52- 646-178-3507 **www.hotelpuntamorro.com**	Expensive to muy expensive	TVs	Yes	Restaurant Bar Pool Jacuzzi	All-suites hotel about 2-1/2 km north of Ensenada. Continental breakfast included. Kitchens, patios, fireplaces and ocean views. Good romantic getaway.
Quintas Papagaya Resort 011-52-646-174-4575 or 4980 www.quintaspapagayo.com	Moderate	Some TVs	Yes	Restaurant Pool Jacuzzi	About 3km outside Ensenada to the north. Older, but cheaper than the other big hotels in Ensenada. Close to boats to Todos Santos. Some kitchenettes. Suites have balconies over the ocean.
San Miguel Village RV Park Tel. 011-52-646-174-7948	Inexpens- ive			Restaurant Bar Camping	Right on its namesake break. All hook ups, showers (cold), restrooms.
San Nicolas Hotel & Casico Tel. 858-427-0634 (US), 011-52- 646-176-1901 or 02 www.sannicolashotel.com	Expensive	A/C, Cable	Yes	Restaurant Bar/disco Pool Spa Guarded parking	Tourist hotel in town near the PEMEX on Lopez Mateo. Somewhat dark and dingy, especially for the price. And it's noisy, too, with the disco and all. But the rooms are good sized.

Estero Beach

Best known for the family oriented resort hotel here, rather than the
beachbreaks or rivermouth sandbar surf. Estero is Spanish for estuary, which
in Surfer means surfable waves, and often with great shape. And sure
enough, there are sandbars out there, some quite a ways out there, and
sometimes with good lefts and rights. Exposure is to the west and northwest,
with waves from the south completely blocked, so this is primarily a winter
break, but with a big enough south the swells wrap in. If no waves, fish the
estuary. And if you don't fish, Estero is a personal watercraft (Jet Skis) haven.
Estero Beach is easy to find. Heading south out of Ensenada simply look for
and follow the signs. Estero Beach is not a great surf destination, especially in
the summer. And it's private, so you can't just drive up and check out the
surf. But if you stay at the Estero Beach Hotel Resort…

Where to Stay for Estero Beach

The best way in is through the resort hotel, so you may as well stay there.
That or park your RV or tent. Long-term RV spaces available.

Lodging Name	Rates	A/C, TV	Credit Cards	Facilities	Comments
Estero Beach Hotel Resort Tel. 619-335-1145 (US), 818-336-9377 (US), 011-52-646-176-6225, 30 or 35 www.hotelesterobeach.com	Moderate to muy expensive	Cable TV	Yes	Restaurant Bar Tennis Playground Volleyball Boat ramp RV park	On the beach. Suites have kitchenettes. Rents kayaks, wave runners and other fun stuff.

Just south of Ensenada is a checkpoint where you will be expected to show
your tourist papers. (If you don't already have your visa pick one up from the
immigration office — *Servicios Migrarios* — located on your left as you enter
Ensenada from the north, which if you're near this southern checkpoint is up
to an hour drive away.) They rarely ask for them at this checkpoint, especially
when heading south, but those teenagers with machine guns in the bunkers
next to the road are reason enough to be prepared. When heading north into
Ensenada, expect to be stopped and have your vehicle searched. And since
they are searching heavily, expect delays. They are looking for drugs and
other stuff, whatever that might be.

The coast between Ensenada to the north and the town of Todos Santos to the
south near Cabo has little in the way of facilities for casual tourists and
nothing for anyone requiring upscale comforts. If you came looking for Baja,
this is it.

LA BUFADORA TO EL ROSARIO

No matter how much time you plan for your drive through Ensenada, always add another half hour, as there is always more traffic than you would expect. But you already know that, now that you are…

Leaving Ensenada going south you will pass through a military checkpoint which, among other things, signals that you are entering a different world — what most like to think of as the real Baja. This is where it changes from San Diego's low-rent suburb to BAJA. The checkpoint is (actually was) at Maneadora — an odd place with campgrounds, a little store, restrooms (*sanitarios*) and other things that seem out of place. (It recently moved south a few miles to just where you go through the hills. This could be temporary just to trip up smugglers, but who knows.) Technically, you are expected to present your tourist permit or visa, but they rarely ask for it. You are also supposed to present papers when returning through the checkpoint, but there's a better chance they'll ask you on the trip north. And you are likely to get your vehicle searched, so don't test that part of the system.

As you head south of Ensenada travel becomes more difficult. It is harder to reach or find the surf breaks as access roads can be rough, steep, long or all three. There are already few signs for directions in Baja and even fewer here. Ocean conditions also get more challenging, too, with higher winds and lower water temps, until you get to Baja Sur.

This is also where many of the horror stories of tragic highway deaths originate. Rule #1: Do not make this drive at night. The truck drivers are tequila'd out, and know they will win any confrontation with an oncoming car. To them it's like bull fighting; they are the matadors and you are the bull. *Hey-ey, torrrr-oooo*. The bull always loses. So, when El Matador challenges you with a head-on you will likely decide to avoid a certain death by pulling onto the shoulder. Then, in your best Homer Simpson voice you will yell, "Doh!" as you fly off into oblivion. Because there are almost no shoulders. Rule #1: Don't drive at night.

Despite warnings about other drivers, your most likely collision will be with livestock, and once again, at night. But this time the bull wins. Or maybe it's a draw. But you lose in a draw anyhow. Rule #1.

Another thing: The universal signal for "It is all clear up ahead; go ahead and pass me," is flashing a left blinker. Do not trust it. The drivers mean well, but they have a different interpretation of "It is all clear up ahead." Clear is relative. And unfortunately, that signal still means "I'm turning left," too. So if the driver ahead slows down while signaling left, don't pass. Wait to see if they are turning left or helping you get around.

La Bufadora

Just around the southern tip of Punta Banda. Take the turnoff at the north end of Maneadero, on to Mex 23. Bufadora is a tourist spot with a visitor center — and you know what that means: Toilets! Camping with RV hook-ups and other facilities can be found at the La Jolla Beach Camp. Other campgrounds nearby with lesser facilities. Not really a surf break, but Bufadora offers another option for getting to Islas de Todos Santos via the La Bufadora Dive Shop, which offers surf trips.

Bahía Soledad

Friends had told me about this hidden bay; then Ensenada resident Josh Hansen wrote me a nice letter describing the break. Situated between Punta Banda to the north and Santo Tomás to the south, west-facing Bahía Soledad is mostly sandy beachbreak catching swells from most directions. With winter rains the sand builds up on the north end for solid, thick rights. To get here you need to drive toward Boca de Santo Tomás but take the turnoff to the north before you reach the beach. You'll need a 4x4 or a truck with good clearance. Or if you have an airplane there's a landing strip fronting this mile-long sandy beach. Either way, you will definitely have the surf to yourself. No one goes here. Except Josh.

Boca de Santo Tomás

There is no coast road between Ensenada and Punta Santo Tomás. It is pretty much a destination unto itself (unless you decide to check out Soledad to the north). So if you are coming up from Punta San José, the same holds true — you have to drive back to the Mexico 1. You can try the dirt track up from Punta San José if you have a mountain goat-like four-wheel drive, but it's sketchy. You will probably make it to the little fishing village after a bit of crawling up and down the narrow dirt road, and there is a little surf to be found there, but the track (I hesitate to call it a road) deteriorates further after that. So while it's just a few kilometers to Punta China at that point, your best bet is the long drive back out through Punta San José to Puerto Santo Tomás on Mexico 1. Ask anyone and they'll tell you not to try.

The turnoff from Mexico 1 is clearly marked with a *"PTO. STO.TOMAS"* sign seen from both directions. The drive in is about 16.5 miles—the road sign says 33 kilometers—and is easy to navigate, as the dirt road is wide and smooth. At some places the road splits in two, with the north fork tracking along the. Take your pick, the roads converge. As you near the Boca de Santo Tomás you will see a sign to turn south to Punta China. Go check it out. There is surf and camping. The actual *"boca"* or La Bocana is the rivermouth of Río Santo Tomás. You will see the estuary as you approach the beach, along with a grassy campground. Continue on and you will find the fish camp, a couple of stores, more camping, RV parking, and some cabins to rent. Head around the point to the northwest and you will see the fishing boats in the bay, eventually reaching the Alamo-esque arch with a sign saying "Real Baja Puerto Santo Tomás", the entrance to the Puerto Santo Tomas Resort.

There's a variety of surf at Santo Tomás—WSW facing sandy beach, reef breaks and right point breaks—with lots of kelp to keep it glassy. Head a bit to the south and you'll get to **Punta China**, with camping and fun surf.

There is also a picturesque little area with a fishing village, some touristy stuff, and nice vacation homes available for rent. Here you will find more camping (showers, toilets), a store, restaurant, cantina and lodging.

Where to Stay for Santo Tomas

There's camping and the Puerto Santo Tomas Resort. The Resort, which is way around to the north side of the bay at the fishing village has a variety of lodging, from cabinas to a "bridal suite", with prices ranging from around $20 daily per person to $1,500 weekly per couple. There's much to do here, from fishing and boating to whale watching and enjoying a nice restaurant. Find them at www.puertosantotomas.com and 011-52-646-154-9415.

Punta San José

A series of right reefs line up for fun, long, workable right point/reef break surf. With big swells the reefs connect for very long rides. But even on smaller swells quick little rights pop up for fun, well-shaped peaks. While known for the rights, there are also good lefts too. Consistent and breaks on nearly all swells with enough size, but faces SW so best on west to south swells. But big winter NW swells wrap in nicely. Gets good offshores, but doesn't need it as the heavy (at times too heavy) kelp and the high cliffs keep the wind damage down when the onshores kick in. The beach itself is mostly rocks and reefs — not much sand.

You can camp on the cliffs over the surf (with the rest of San Diego — this is a favorite weekend getaway). Cliffs, rather than bluffs is the right word as it's a steep drop over the edge to the rocks below, unless you head around the cove to the north near the lighthouse. It is probably not a good place to go camping with small children, or to get boozed up at night. Beach access is not difficult, however, as there are a couple of easy paths down. The camping is basic: All you will find is dirt and outhouses, but local fishermen are right there and stop by to sell lobster.

It's possible to drive the dirt tracks/roads from Punta China in the north, but much depends on the season (winter rains wash the road out), year, your vehicle and skills. Coming from the south is easier. But coming from Mexico 1 is easiest.

On Mexico 1 drive 29 miles south from Ensenada through the Santo Tomás wine-growing valley and into the little hamlet of Santo Tomás. Look for the *"PTO. STO.TOMAS"* road sign with the arrow pointing west. (Buy supplies now because there is nothing but surf at Punta San José.) Fourteen miles from Santo Tomás turn right at a fork in the road — there is a sign — and drive another 10 miles or so until you see other surfers camping at the point. If there is no one there, you will know you are at Punta San José when you see the lighthouse. By the way, if you turn left at that same fork and you will be on your way to Punta Cabras.

Punta Cabras

Nice sandy cove with good reefbreaks and beachbreaks that stay pretty glassy even when there is wind. The fastest way to get here is to come from Punta San Isidro to the south. But you are more likely driving down Mex 1, so the turnoff is in Santo Tomás and the directions are the same as with Punta San José above, except for the left turn at the fork. There should be a sign there. Do not bother trying to find a beach route unless you are coming up from Punta San Isidro. Between Punta San José and Punta Cabras you will have to drive through private, fenced ranches and other obstacles.

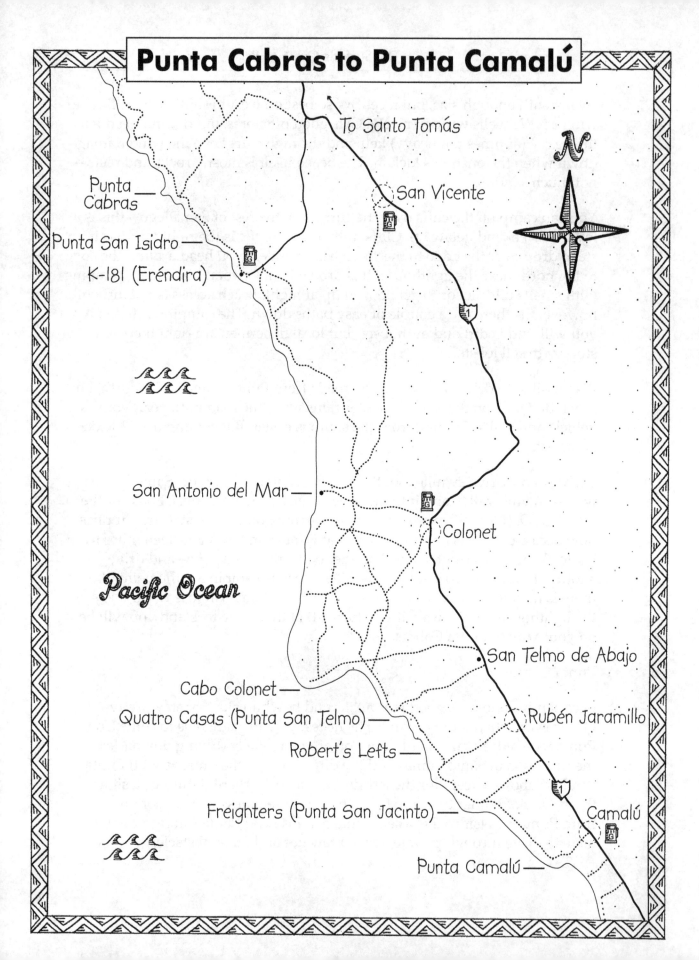

Punta Cabras to Punta Camalú

To Santo Tomás

San Vicente

Punta Cabras

Punta San Isidro

K-181 (Eréndira)

San Antonio del Mar

Colonet

Pacific Ocean

San Telmo de Abajo

Cabo Colonet

Quatro Casas (Punta San Telmo)

Rubén Jaramillo

Robert's Lefts

Freighters (Punta San Jacinto)

Camalú

Punta Camalú

Now if you follow a good map you will find that the beach marked with the hamlet of Punta Cabras and bordered on the north by the point named Punta Cabras is actually not the surf beach known to us Gringos as Punta Cabras. There is some surf here, but it's not nearly as good or consistent. You can camp here, too, and get to know the locals. It is a popular campground for Mexican families.

When driving up from Punta San Isidro, you will have to pass that beach by driving inland a bit (you can't make it by driving on the roads closest to the beach) north to where the road heads back to the beach in what is marked on maps as "La Punta del Cañon de Santa Cruz," or "Bahía Almejas." Look for camping surfers, or just plain good waves.

Lots of San Diego gringos camp here on weekends, just like Punta San José and other spots around here. It is a pretty safe camping area because of that. The only facilities are flat dirt and an outhouse.

Punta San Isidro

Beach and reefbreaks spread out from the fishing village of Puerto San Isidro north, with the best surf in the coves around the point where Coyote Cal's sits. Camping on your own along the bluffs north of the point—no facilities, but nice, picturesque, close-to-the-water camping—or at campgrounds like at Castro's Place near Puerto San Isidro toward Eréndira. You can also stay at Coyote Cal's (see below). Follow the directions to Punta Cabras and take the coast road south, or better still, drive up from Eréndira—it's much faster. The road along the beach here is good, and right next to the beach.

K-181 (Eréndira)

When driving down from the north on the 1D you will see a bunch of signs for the Eréndira area, including Coyote Cal's, Malibu Beach Sur RV Park, and the smaller but still visible sign for Eréndira ("E.J. Eréndira 20"). Take that road. It is one of the best beach access roads you will find in Baja—it's paved and a short, 20 to 30 minute drive. If you try to find Eréndira by coming up from San Antonio del Mar you will probably get lost many times over; same for driving in from San Vicente. In fact, for the most part those roads don't actually get past the farms. Once you get to Eréndira you will find a bustling little community with pretty much everything you need. The town is bigger than most you pass driving down the 1D.

K-181/Eréndira is a rocky reef area with lots of reefbreaks, a few beachbreaks, many with good lefts, some rights, and kelp beds to help keep things glassy. The breaks are in the area to the north, near **Punta San Isidro** (Coyote Cal's). To the south are the rivermouth beachbreaks (Boca Eréndira or Boca de Río) and the cobblestone beaches of **Malibu Beach Sur**, with fun to big surf, depending on the swell and nice, white-sand beaches. Best on winter northwests, but surf all year round as this area faces WSW. On weekends the locals come out in droves for family beach picnics and camping, especially to the north around Punta San Isidro.

Where to Stay

Camping, camping, camping, a motel, Castro's fish camp (San Isidro) and Coyote Cal's. Coyote Cal's is a gringo-owned, good-times lodging that's sort of a combo bed & breakfast/hostel/hotel with campgrounds. Inexpensive and interesting. There is also a basic but clean motel just on the beach side of the town of Eréndira aptly named Hotel Eréndira. Other cabañas and places are available for rent, too.

Lodging Name	Rates	A/C, TV	Credit Cards	Facilities	Comments
Coyote Cal's Tel. 888-670-2252 (US) www.coyotecals.com	Inexpensive	No A/C, TV in rec room	Yes	Bar Game room	Walk to surf. Rates include breakfast. Fun, gringo-owned place on cliff over the ocean north of Erendira at Punta San Isidro. Off-road motorcycle and hiking tours, whale and dolphin watching, fishing, surfing, mountain biking.
Hotel Eréndira	Inexpensive	No	No	None	Basic motel accommodations if you just need a shower and a bed.
Malibu Beach Sur	Cheap	No	No	RV park Camping	Basic camping and RV sites with surf and a white sand beach out front.

San Antonio Del Mar

Here's another San Antonio Del Mar, but unlike its neighbor near the border, this one is not private. (Mexico and Central America like to recycle names, using the same ones repeatedly, e.g. Todos Santos, Playa Blanca, Playa Negra and San Antonio Del Mar.) San Antonio del Mar is a large, spread out settlement bordering a big estuary. Camping ($3/night) and RV parking without hookups. To get here take the turnoff from Mexico 1D at about Km 126 just north of the town of Colonet and just before you reach the bridge (*puente*). You will find the beach after about seven miles or so; it's due west of Colonet (aka Collnet). Get gas at the Pemex here.

San Antonio del Mar is just one stop along this long, sandy, west-facing stretch of beach with tons of lonely beachbreaks. Fully exposed to all swells, so there's always surf. Explore the area and you will just find more, better and lonelier breaks (if the latter is even possible). You will also likely get lost, so be sure to have lots of gas and bring that extra can. As you head south along this beach toward Cabo Colonet the cliffs get taller and steeper so the beach becomes more difficult to reach. With the right vehicle you can drive on the beach.

Cabo Colonet Through San Quintin Advice

This stretch from Colonet (a.k.a. Colnet) through San Quintin should be marked with "Beware. You are entering a high crime area." Meth-heads, banditos and all sorts of bad guys patrol these towns and beaches and prey on the campers too dumb to park themselves in established campgrounds and other well-inhabited areas. There's a ton of easily accessible surf here and beyond, so there's no need to play "I'm going feral" by setting up your own away-from-it-all camp. You should head south of El Rosario for that.

Cabo Colonet

Right, well-shaped point at the north end of Bahía Colonet and at the base of the steep, dramatic headland. Needs a good-sized swell to start working. With good-sized west to southwest swells you can luck into some nice peelers hugging the cliff. Truth be told, it rarely breaks, but when it does, it can peel perfectly for quite a ways, and it's a long paddle out, too (or cliff-hugging rock-hopping walk out). There are also occasional beach breaks in the cove and increasingly more waves to be found as you head south out from the swell-blocking headland. From the town of Colonet it's about an eight-mile drive to Bahía Colonet, at which point you can head north out the point or south to Cuatro Casas. You'll find the road just south of town; the road itself heads mostly south to the beach. At the north corner of the beach at the base of the headland you will find the Pinedas Fish Camp. Colonet has been on the *Escalera Nautica* death list for years. The plan is to turn Bahía Colonet into a $4 billion port, the largest in Mexico and the third-largest in the world. The port would transform Colonet from a sleepy town of 2,500 to a metropolis of 200,000, and the surf would disappear, of course. Since Cabo Colonet rarely breaks, that might not mean much for surfing here, but it could be the end of the better, more popular Cuatro Casas, the next break to the south.

Cuatro Casas/Punta San Telmo

"Then from a vantage pont high on a mesa, we spotted a horseshoe bay. We could see the fine, rolling lines of the south swell… On top of the plateau, 20 feet above the water, stood four fishermen's huts made of driftwood, tin cans and cardboard…Cuatro Casas…four houses. The given name fit the isolated beauty of the spot." – Greg MacGillivray, "In Darkest Baja," *Surfer* 1968 (The quote was actually found in *The Surfer's Journal* article *Light in Darkest Baja: Kent Layton's Boat Ranch*, Spring 2001.)

Probably the best-known and most-crowded break between San Miguel and Cabo. The reason for its popularity is a bit of a mystery to most, except maybe old-timers. It is certainly a good right reef/point when on, like at 20 other Baja breaks, but many of those breaks are better, more consistent and less famous. Cuatro Casas breaks best on souths, but bigger wests and northwests also provide good surf. The terrain and kelp keep the wind damage down, so it stays glassier than other spots, and it gets damn windy in this stretch of Baja. The cove faces southwest, but the point juts way out there so lots of swell can get in. There are mostly longboards in the lineup here.

One reason for the popularity is that it has been written up in the surf press since the 1960s. That, and the campgrounds right over the break, AKA the Boat Ranch. Get the article (available for download) from *The Surfer's Journal* to learn all about the Boat Ranch. Or just go. You can camp or park for $5/day and you will get to experience the Boat Ranch and use the outhouses, too.

It is easy enough to find Cuatro Casas once you get down to the beach, but picking the right road down can be confusing. Try this: About 12 kilometers south of the town of Colonet you will find San Telmo. About 9/10's of a mile south of the San Telmo PEMEX you will find a turnoff that goes through a few farms and finds its way to the beach (about 5½ to 6 miles). The turnoff is a little hard to find, but it's just past the "Abarrotes Ormart" store on your right and across from "Estetica Y Novedades Marilu." Once you get near the beach take the best-looking dirt road to the south and you will run into the back side of Punta San Telmo, or Cuatro Casas. You can also use the directions above for Cabo Colonet and just drive south from there. (There are also some uncrowded waves along the way.)

The dirt roads in this whole area have improved dramatically—graded to a very good condition, so getting a bit lost is not a disaster.

Camping was the rule for decades, but Cuatro Casas has gone "upscale" with the opening of the Cuatro Casas Hostel (www.cuatrocasashostel.com) where you can get a bed ($15) or a private room ($40). It has much of whatever you need, plus a pool for skating. They serve meals and have outdoor showers available. Not quite a hotel, but much more comfortable than a tent. Or maybe a retired boat.

Whatever you do, don't camp out away from this settlement. Crime is zero in the campgrounds/hostel. You're on your own outside. And there has been a lot of crime in this area, from basic robberies to sexual assaults.

Robert's Lefts

Goofy foots should head south when they get tired of going backside (or the crowd) at Cuatro Casas to a stretch of cobblestone beach and a break called Robert's Lefts. Make that a couple breaks. I'm not really sure which one is the real Robert's Lefts. There is one spot just south of the fishing boats that line up with the house inland about a half a kilometer—or (probably) the second set of fishing boats driving along the shore from Cuatro Casas. Another is right in front of the crucifix-marked gravesite. The reefbreak here starts working with bigger swells, and likes northwests, but it faces southwest and picks up all swells. There are a couple of A-frames here. (Yes, Robert's Lefts has rights.) Offshore kelp beds help keep the midday wind chop down. It is never crowded, and the waves are good. Often better and more powerful than either of the more popular point breaks nearby.

Shipwrecks, Freighters, Rincon de Baja or Punta San Jacinto

For once you will be absolutely sure where you are, because a beached freighter, the Isla del Carmen—not that you can see the name on the rusted out hull—is right there in the lineup marking the spot. Right pointbreak needing a good-sized swell to get exciting, and with a decent swell it peels for over 100 yards. Freighters is a pretty forgiving wave (i.e., it's mostly mushy), although there are sometimes bigger more challenging waves breaking outside. Considered a kook wave by some, or a nice relaxing surf by others.

As mentioned before, it gets windy around here, but the point and kelp keep these waves protected. Catches most swells, but other nearby spots are bigger and better on northwests. Best on south swells, but a good option on the really big northwest swells for a fun surf option.

South of the point, between Punta San Jacinto and Camalú, are a lot of surf options, depending on the swell and tide. On bigger wests and northwests there are outside reefs all over the place, with most of them having better lefts than rights. Those outside reefs are way, way outside, but there's enough surf near shore to keep anyone happy if they're looking for uncrowded surf. Yes, totally deserted, but be careful, as a lack of fellow surfers doesn't mean all is well. Crime is an issue here.

Freighters ain't what it used to be. If you haven't been there in a few years you will be shocked. Where there once was one little structure at the point, there are now dozens of homes, trailers and a surf camp lining the shore making the access more difficult (i.e., private) and the lineup more crowded. Camping and parking around the north side of the point is $5/day, and you are not even in front of the break. The trailer owners rent their lots from the locals, so I suppose you can too if you want in on the privatization.

Punta San Jacinto is easy to find from any direction. It is in plain view as you look north from the north side of Puntal Camalú. And just as easy to see when heading south along the beach from Cuatro Casas. It is even easier to find from the 1D because there are signs pointing the way, which is a real treat in Baja. From the 1D you will see the signs just as you leave the unmarked village of Abarca, which is less than three miles south of the marked village of Rubén Jaramillo. The signs say "Parador Turistico/Punta de San Jacinto/Campgrounds Surfing/Cold Beer/3 ½ miles." Just drive about 3 ½ miles (per the sign) to the ocean from there.

Where to Stay for Shipwrecks, Roberts Lefts, Camalu

In the old days camping was the only option, but now there is a surf camp and a burgeoning trailer city. The surf camp is Baja Surf Adventures—a resort-style surf camp that's right in front of the surf. Great for beginners because they have lessons and Freighters is an easy wave. They also book trips to Central and Southern Baja, Mainland Mexico and Central America. The fact that there is now a surf camp is not the only reason not to camp. Crime has become a huge issue in this whole area. (See the story on Pat

Weber in Camping earlier in this book.) Thievery, armed gun-in-your-face robberies, and assaults. Go online and you will see all sorts of stories. Be aware and be smart. And if you want to camp, it's probably safer to head back to the Boat Ranch at Quatros Casas.

Lodging Name	Rates	A/C, TV	Credit Cards	Facilities	Comments
Baja Surf Adventures Surf Camp Tel. 800-HAV-SURF www.bajasurfadventures.com	Moderate (cuz meals are included)	No	No	Bar Kayaks Wi-fi Satellite TV Board rentals	All-inclusive surf camp. Rates include meals. Separate men's and women's restrooms. Surf lessons. Great for beginners. Must book in advance—no walk-ins.
La Cueva del Pirata Tel. 011-52 (616) 159-6575 http://vagabonders-supreme.net/Pirata.htm	Moderate	No	No	Restaurant Bar Camping with hook-ups	Nice hotel with restaurant and bar overlooking Punta Camalu. Nicest hotel in the area.

Rincon de Baja

There is lots of confusion about this one. I go with the version where Punta San Jacinto is Rincon de Baja or Little Rincon, so look above for the description. Others, like *Wave-finder Mexico* ascribe the name to the point at Punta Camalú. Ask the really old-timers and they'll tell you it was Rincon de Baja before the freighter beached itself on the reef, starting the controversy.

No matter, as mentioned above, drive along the beach road south between Punta San Jacinto and Punta Camalú and look for surf. It won't be hard to find. You'll likely to find some great, uncrowded surf as there are a bunch of reef and beachbreaks on this easily-accessed cobblestone stretch. The dirt track along the cliff is sandy, but good. After a short drive you will reach Punta Camalú, and that's a whole other story.

Punta Camalú

The fourth in this series of right points between Colonet and Camalu, Punta Camalu is a big headland with a ton of waves, complemented by a bunch of reef and beachbreaks up and down the cove. More consistent than its neighbor to the north, Cuatro Casas, and stays just as glassy as it's protected from the wind by the point and the kelp, but it's usually small and pretty mushy. (None of the points along this strip are hollow.) Camalú does take in all swells, with all sorts of reefs breaking when the bigger wests appear, like the long right peeler that breaks off the reef right in front of where the access road meets the beach, not to mention the reefs at the end of the point, but as mentioned, it's usually small. Basically, there are tons of waves here of varying quality, from OK to really good, and it's never crowded.

It should be more crowded since Camalú is close to the highway and access is easy, but the crime in the area and the fact that it always looks smaller than it's probably puts a damper on things. It does get crowded on weekends with locals, but they're on the sandy beach, so it's not totally isolated. And the hotel/restaurant built around 2003, the appropriately named La Cueva del Pirata (the Pirate's Cove) gives it less of an isolated feel, too. (See Where to Stay for Shipwrecks, etc. above.

The quickest access is from the Transpeninsular Highway, where you'll turn southwest at the traffic signal just north of the PEMEX station in the town of Camalú. As you approach the beach you will sometimes see what looks like a hundred dudes in the water. They are pelicans, not surfers. You can drive right down onto the beach, but it's easier to reach the reef by driving around to the point. Camalu is a pretty big town, so it has food and most supplies.

Playas San Ramón

Long stretch of unremarkable beachbreaks, but it's definitely uncrowded. The access road from Mex 1 is near Km 172 just south of Vicente Guerrero; just look for a dirt road going west. After about four kilometers or so you will reach the dunes. Camp pretty much anywhere around here.

La Salina

If you head towards Playas San Ramón from further south (see San Quintín on the *Baja California Almanac* map) following the "Marina La Salina" signs you will arrive at the beach at La Salina. You will find the waves. Tons of empty beach breaks. Very secluded.

Playas San Ramón to Casas

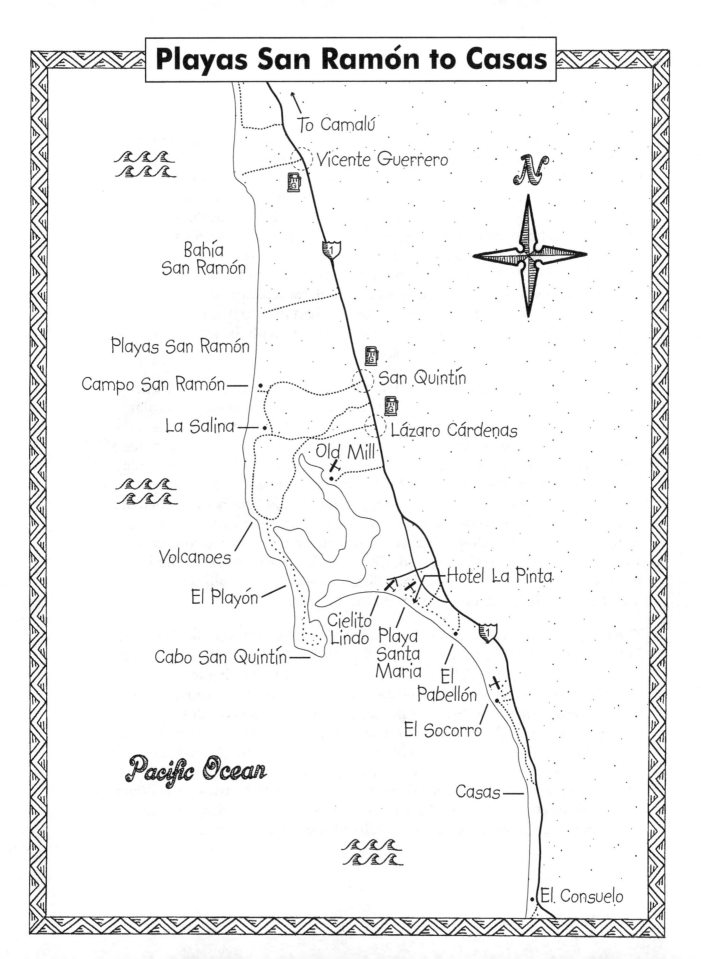

Cabo San Quintín

If you have a sand-worthy 4-wheel drive you are hereby invited to venture out to this great, uncrowded, sand-bottom, wrap-around right pointbreak. (Actually, two pointbreaks.) Difficult access and a long drive out to the points, but that's what makes it great. That, and the offshores that blow in the face of the waves as they wrap around the point into the bay at Punta Entrada. Another option for getting out here is taking a boat—probably your own. Paying a fisherman to take you out here will be expensive as this is a sportfishing area and that has driven up the prices. There are lots of sportfishing operations, so check around or look for a panga. It's still a long trip out, but you won't get stuck in the sand. (I had to help two vehicles dig out on my last trip out here.) Best on west swells. As with the rest of the area, there's good fishing, and (well-fed) sharks.

To get to Cabo San Quintín and its neighbors look for the *Zona Turistica de Atractivos Naturales Bajia Falsa Parque Volcanico* sign on the Transpeninsular Highway. Heading south there will be a bunch of trees on the right side (That's an army base.) just before you reach the turnoff. You should also see a blue airport sign just before reaching the turnoff. (Reset your odometer.) Stay on the wide, gravel road. It is a pretty scenic drive cruising around the volcanoes and the back bay, but be sure you have good tires because there are a lot of sharp volcanic rocks on the road. You will know you are still on the right road and getting close when you reach the home of the world famous warrior oysters, marked by the sign "Ostiones Guerrero." At about the 10 mile point you will reach the fishing village "Los Volcanes," although there are no signs telling you that. Turn right for the surf.

The water temps in this area can be roughly 10 to 15 degrees colder than San Diego – even colder than other parts of Baja Norte. The wind blows hard out of the northwest starting late morning most of the year, helping to further cool things off. In fact, this is one of the windiest parts of Baja. You'll figure that out when you see all the trees pointing inland as you drive down the Transpeninsular Highway. That wind also drops the air temperature, so long sleeves or light jackets are often in order. San Quintín (with Lázaro Cárdenas) itself is the biggest town in the area, with everything you need including restaurants, hotels and banking. There are also plenty of airstrips here. When driving through San Quintín plan on encountering traffic, adding to your drive time. San Quintín itself is about 120 miles south of Ensenada.

If heading to the San Quintín area you might look up Captain Kelly Catian at K&M Offshore Sportfishing (try from USA 949-370-6532, or Baja 011-52-616-103-6704). He has run sportfishing operations in this area for years, but he surfs too, so he also runs K&M Surf Adventures.

I suppose it's pretty well known by now, but it deserves mention anyhow: San Quintín has a lot of crime. So be extra careful.

Volcanoes

If you make the trek out to the points at Cabo San Quintín, you will probably see some good surf along the way. And given the difficult drive to the end of the cape, you might just consider checking out the breaks at Volcanoes or El Playón (next). Volcanoes is a variety of lava-rock reef breaks — good, juicy and for experts only. The "experts only" warning probably is not necessary, as the sharp lava reefs speak for themselves. Volcanoes stretches from the reef/point at the north end of the fishing village, Los Volcanes, along the south to the reef/point just north of the fishing village at El Playón. There are anywhere from three to five different reefs firing at any given time. Eventually they will all get their own names, but probably not for a long time as no one surfs here. This whole area has good exposure, facing west, so it picks up a lot of swell.

There is always something to surf along this stretch, and you don't need a 4-wheel drive to surf the reefs near the village. But don't even think about driving south out toward the Cabo San Quintín points without one. And bring booties as some of the breaks are reached only by walking over a sharp lava rock reef.

El Playón

As you head south out to Cabo San Quintín you will trudge up through the volcano hills on the sandy trails eventually (it's about three miles) descending into a fishing village at the north end of a long sandy beach known as El Playón or West Medano Beach. This is a beautiful beach that's part of a protected reserve (you are supposed to pay $2 at the entrance) with a ton of well-shaped beachbreak. It faces west so it picks up a ton of swell, and there is no one there. Camping is allowed.

On the way to El Playón you will come upon a house sitting out on a lava reef point. Here you will find a little right that's usually glassy as the prevailing wind blows somewhat offshore and it's surrounded by kelp. Actually, it's smothered in kelp. Bring booties for the walk over the sharp lava reef.

Playa Santa Maria or Cielito Lindo

Miles of southwest facing, rather ordinary beachbreaks. Blocked by Cabo San Quintín from northwest and most west swells, but the better ones get in. Totally uncrowded, but that's mostly due to the rather ordinary quality of the surf. Best on higher tides where you can sometimes find racy, barreling shoulders, so long as the surf doesn't get much more than a couple of feet overhead, which is when the whole beach closes out. There is camping in the area, along with lodging like the Cielito Lindo and the Desert Inn Hotel (formerly La Pinta). Cielito Lindo has a decent restaurant and bar, along with RV park, campgrounds and sportfishing, but it's set back from the beach so it's a long walk or a short drive. Rooms with two beds are $45/night, and the RV park is $5/night. The Desert Inn Hotel is part of the "upscale" chain of Baja hotels and has a restaurant, bar and tennis. Kind of desolate, but it's a decent hotel right on the beach and the upstairs rooms have great beach views. La Pinta is 2 1/2 miles west of Hwy 1. Follow the signs.

A little ways south of the Desert Inn Hotel along the beach and one mile west of Highway 1 is a big campground, El Pabellon RV Park & Campgrounds. The beachbreak surf is mediocre or worse, as all of this area, but if you are looking for a more "civilized" campground, this is one. There are hot showers and toilets in two separate bathhouses. There are also lots of sinks for cleaning fish. The price is $5/night for parking along the beach without water or sewer hookups, and more for a space with water and sewer connections. And there is a cool whale skeleton to wow the kids (which is really why I have highlighted El Pabellon). For the old timers, this place used to be called Honey's. It is easy to find from the highway as there are at least two big signs pointing the way.

Where to Stay Around San Quintín

If you are heading out to Cabo San Quintín, Volcanoes or El Playón, plan to camp. Otherwise, you can stay either in town or in the backbay at or by the Old Mill Hotel as the drive out and back takes awhile. The Old Mill Hotel is on the bay with a boat ramp and kitchenettes. Popular with the fishing and dirt bike crowds. It is a drive or a boat trip to any surf from The Old Mill as it's tucked away in the backbay, but it's a nice place to relax with an open courtyard facing the bay, volcanoes and spectacular sunsets. It is also a pretty good deal for the area when you compare the quality of the rooms at Cielito Lindo (although the food is good there) and the prices at Desert Inn. Make reservations during the summer; you can probably slip in during the off season. Don Eddie's, another backbay option is great. For RVs check out Campo de Lorenzo—full hookups, bathrooms and showers. Just south of San Quintín are other options. In town right on the Transpeninsular is the Motel Chavéz. Billed as a "family" hotel, it's clean, inexpensive and convenient to the highway. A good choice.

Lodging Name	Rates	A/C, TV	Credit Cards	Facilities	Comments
Desert Inn Hotel Tel. 866-539-0036 (US), 866-599-6674 (US)	Moderate to Expensive	Yes, Yes	Yes	Restaurant Bar Tennis	A sort of upscale place—relatively speaking—in the middle of nowhere, but right on the beach south of San Quintín with some beachbreak out front. TVs. Best hotel in the area.
Don Eddie's Landing Tel. 011-52-616-165-6061, 011-52-616-165-6062 www.doneddies.com	Moderate	No, Yes	No	Restaurant Bar Catering	Nice place near the Old Mill in back bay. Some rooms have four beds. Sportfishing resort. Great views from restaurant and bar.
El Pabellón Trailer Park RV	Inexpensive	No, No	No	Hook ups-sewer only	South of San Quintín. Water, showers, restrooms. Right on the beach with beachbreaks out front.
Motel Chavéz Tel. 011-52-616-165-2005	Inexpensive	Fans, Yes	Yes	Restaurant Bar	In town. TVs. No a/c. Clean, nice, good beds, good choice.
Old Mill Hotel Tel. 800-479-7962 (US), 877-800-4081 (US), 800-025-5141 (Mex toll free) e. oldmill@telnor.net	Moderate	Fans, No	Yes	RV hook ups Camping Boat launch	Away from the surf in the back bay. Some rooms have kitchens and fireplaces. Sportfishing operation. Long-time favorite of the fishing crowd. Noisy at night as the fishing crowd tends to party hardy. Tell the owner Jim we said hola. Great place.
Rancho Cielito Lindo Tel. 619-593-2252 (US), 011-52-616-162-1021 www.cielitolindo.8m.com	Moderate	Yes, No	No	Restaurant Bar RV park Camping Boat launch	Away from it all but within walking distance of the beach south of San Quintín. Large, well-lit but shabby rooms. Sportfishing operation. Electricity shut off during midday. As with La Pinta, a bit overpriced for what you get.
Rancho Sereno Bed & Breakfast Tel. 909-982-7087 (US)	Moderate		No	Restaurant	Quaint, three-room bed & breakfast west of town.

El Socorro

El Socorro is a gringo settlement with an airstrip just off the highway. Uncrowded rights and lefts breaking off reefs at the rivermouth just south of a point. Sand and cobblestone beach with some rocks. Best on wests and souths, taking in lots of swell. The best waves are right in front of the airstrip and rivermouth. Cheap camping on the beach, RV parking and an airstrip right there. There are often some surfers in the water here, but heading south are miles of beach and reefbreaks you can have to yourself. Turn west just north of the bridge (over the riverbed) at Rancho Los Coyotes or El Socorrito. You'll pass the airstrip on your left just before you get to the signs saying you need permission to pass. Sometimes there's someone there, sometimes not. Turn right and drive around to the beach. Or just head south over the bridge and take the first turnoff. It will lead to the cobblestone beach just south of the rivermouth. You can surf right out front, but it's better in front of the rivermouth and the point. The campground here has a toilet. (Woo-hoo!) The trash recycling instruction sign reads: "Plastics, spray cans and polluting stuff take it back to U.S.A." Robberies reported at the campgrounds.

Casas, etc.

Driving south from El Socorro to El Consuelo you will find a long stretch of easily accessed beaches with good, totally uncrowded reefbreaks and beachbreaks. The first version of *The Surf Report* called this "Cuatro Casas," creating some confusion between this and the real Quatros Casas to the north. That's been fixed with the latest edition. One of the many places to turn off with easy access to the surf is just south of the Km 36 marker as you drive down the hill just before the bridge.

A little further south the road turns inland as you transition to the next phase of Baja, where most of the surf breaks are much more difficult to access. This stretch of road is also one of those spots you want to avoid driving at night, as it's narrow, winding and there's little margin for error.

MILITARY CHECKPOINT NOTE: The military checkpoint between San Quintín and El Rosario can be a major pain. For some reason, the soldiers at this checkpoint perform much more thorough and unfriendly searches. They take time and mess up your stuff, but don't cop an attitude as it will just cause more grief. This routine seems to be most predominant on the northbound lane.

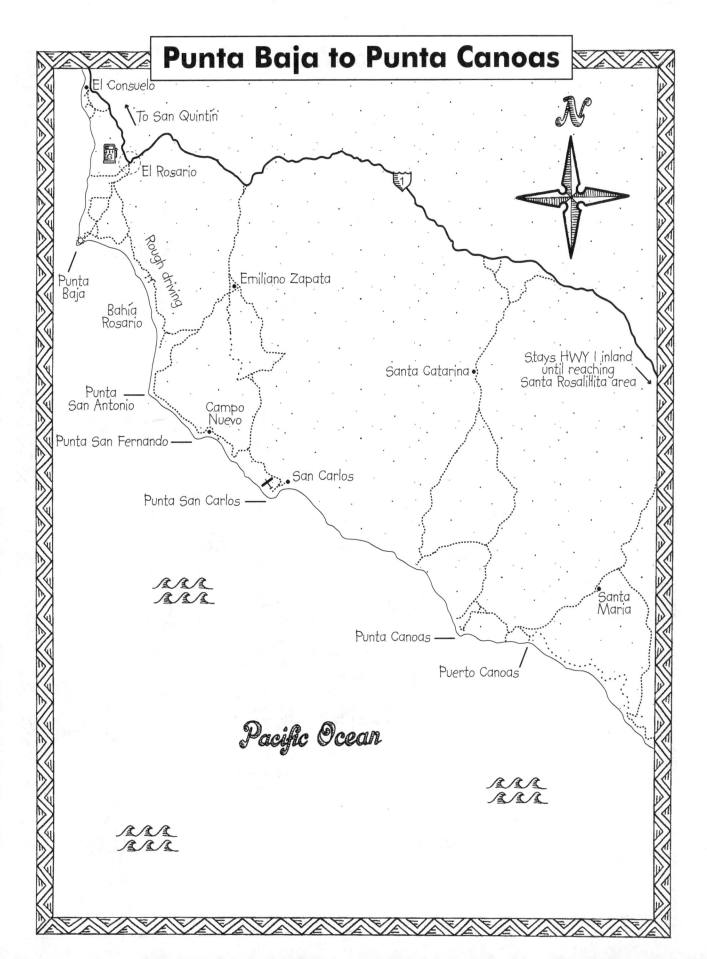

Punta Baja to Punta Canoas

El Consuelo

To San Quintín

El Rosario

Punta Baja

Rough driving

Bahía Rosario

Emiliano Zapata

Santa Catarina

Stays HWY I inland
until reaching
Santa Rosalillita area

Punta
San Antonio

Campo
Nuevo

Punta San Fernando

San Carlos

Punta San Carlos

Santa
Maria

Punta Canoas

Puerto Canoas

Pacific Ocean

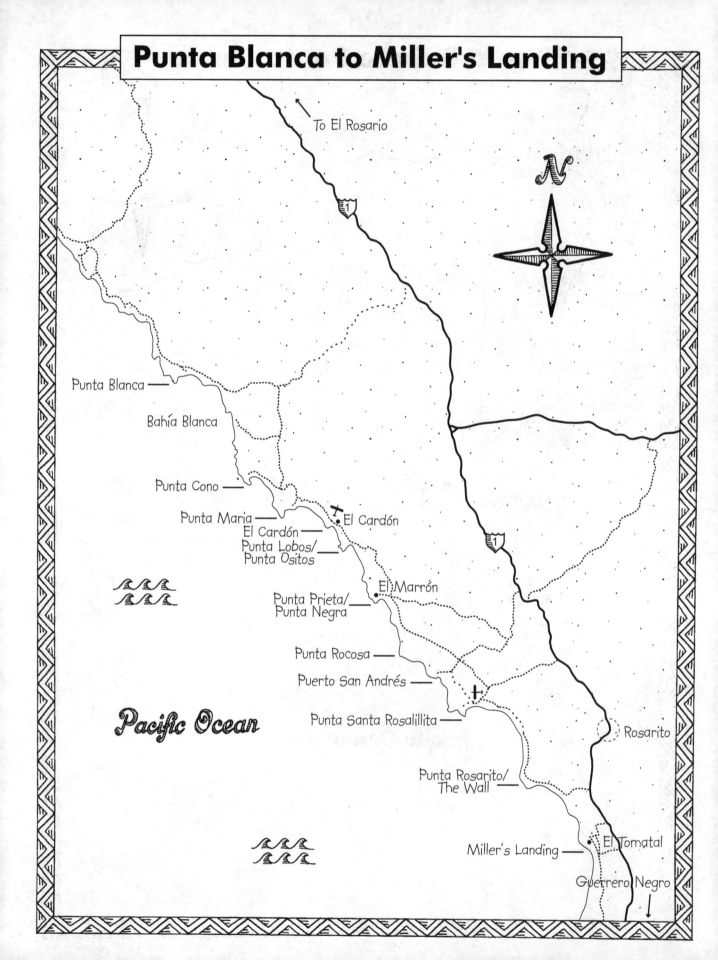

Punta Blanca to Miller's Landing

N

To El Rosario

Punta Blanca

Bahía Blanca

Punta Cono

Punta Maria

El Cardón

El Cardón

Punta Lobos/
Punta Ositos

El Marrón

Punta Prieta/
Punta Negra

Punta Rocosa

Puerto San Andrés

Punta Santa Rosalillita

Rosarito

Punta Rosarito/
The Wall

Pacific Ocean

Miller's Landing

El Tomatal

Guerrero Negro

Punta Baja to Cedros Island

You probably noticed that the kilometer road markers heading south reset themselves to zero in San Quintín at around the turnoff to the Old Mill Hotel. Consider that foreshadowing, as everything resets from here.

Just as Baja changes dramatically heading south out of Ensenada, it goes to a new level after reaching El Rosario. Consider that, up until 1973 this was the end of the road, literally. That year the Transpeninsular Highway was completed, paving the way to the modern Baja era.

As the road turns inland it gets difficult to reach many of the breaks, sometimes requiring a big commitment. If you are committed, you will do what it takes to get to these spots, which means investing time and accepting getting lost. A lot. Be prepared with supplies – food, water and gas – as help is a long way away.

You will know you are getting close to El Rosario when you reach the military checkpoint. Just as you enter town from the north you will see a PEMEX on the left side of the highway. (If you are heading further south, get gas now. It is a long way to the next gas stop, Cataviña, and that station doesn't always have gas.) Just past the PEMEX is the legendary Mama Espinosa's restaurant where you can load up on their excellent lobster burritos (for a few more bucks than you are used to in Mexico, but a portion of the profits go to a local orphanage) and the La Cabaña Motel, owned by the same folks. This is not a bad place to stop for the night, either, as the nearest surf to the south is a long ways away. Except Punta Baja.

Punta Baja

A long, rocky right point with reefs in the bay. Souths and solid west/northwest swells all work. Waves off the point wrap around toward the north so it's offshore here more than most spots, which is pretty nice. But it also gets foggy, and those winds can make camping uncomfortable. The surf is spread out along this appendix-shaped point that is also home to a fish camp. (Fish camp means there are fishermen to sell you fresh fish and lobsters.) The word about these fun, forgiving rights has been spread far and wide over the years, but there are also lefts further inside the bay. Needs good-sized west or big northwest swell; faces south so all of those swells get in, so it's better in summer.

Compared to the surf breaks to the south, Punta Baja is not that far from the Transpeninsular Highway, about 10 miles, so it's definitely worth checking. If you are driving from the north you will see the turnoff on the right just as you pass Mama Espinosas where the road bends to the left (but you turn right). Set your odometer to zero. Once off the highway you will quickly come to a fork where you will want to go left. You will cross a riverbed that may have a bit of the river, depending on the season (winter wet; summer dry) as you are now driving from the north side of the riverbed to the south. (If you stay on the north side you will find yourself driving to Bocana el Rosario, and you can't get to Punta Baja without backtracking. Then again, it's a rivermouth, so guess what, there's surf.) Some guidebooks will tell you to look for the mission ruins on your right, but don't bother; they are almost impossible to spot. (That's why they call them ruins, there is nothing there. Anyhow, you are in Baja. How does one discern the Ruins from the ruins?) Once you get to the south side of the riverbed the road will turn west (you may even see the tiny sign pointing you to the mission) and pass through a spread out village. At the end of the village (you have gone about three miles now) you will see a tiny wooden sign on the left side of the road pointing to Punta Baja. Take that road, trying to stay on it as best as you can. It gets confusing with all the other roads crossing it. And it's rougher than the road you were just on, but you can still drive it in a car. (Rule of thumb: If the locals can do it you can too.) Eventually, at about 10 miles from the first turnoff, you will see campers on the cliff over the beach, which means you are almost there. Turn south and drive a little ways along the cliff until you reach the fishing village. Now you are there.

Punta Baja is often foggy, so you may have to drive right up to the beach to check the surf. You can also drive south along the beach for more surf and camping, but the road is very rough. So you might want to stock up on gas and supplies in El Rosario before attempting this drive.

Where to Stay for Punta Baja

The choices are motels in El Rosario or camping at the point next to the fishing village. In El Rosario there are three motels, the Baja Cactus Motel, La Cabaña Motel and the Sinai Motel & RV Park (on the main road heading out of town to the south). All of the motels can be noisy at night with the trucks driving through town.

Lodging Name	Rates	A/C, TV	Credit Cards	Facilities	Comments
Baja Cactus Motel Tel. 011-52-616-165-8700 www.bajacactus.com	Moderate	Yes, Satellite TVs	Yes	Security Parking Internet	Next to the Pemex as you come into town from the north. Good value.
La Cabaña Motel/Mama Espinosa's Tel. 011-52-616-165-8770 www.mamaespinoza.com	Moderate	Fans, No	No	Restaurant Laundry Internet	In El Rosario close to the PEMEX. Great restaurant. Slightly more expensive than the Baja Cactus, but it's Mama Espinosa's!
Sanai Motel & RV Park Tel. 011-52-616-165-8818	Inexpensive	No, TVs	No	Restaurant Full hook-ups Laundry	Motel with camping and RV park. RV park has full hook-ups, hot-water showers and (rustic) toilets.

Punta San Antonio

Here's where we start to separate the hardcore from the dilettantes. Access to Punta San Antonio is difficult, but once there you will find a big rocky point with a bunch of reefbreaks. Faces southwest but takes all swells. If you have time, a worthy vehicle, like to camp and fish, and really want to get away from people, then Punta San Antonia is worth the trip. Punta San Antonio doesn't get half the attention of its neighbors to the north and south, so it's that much less crowded. And nothing's crowded around here.

Heading south out of El Rosario look for the Puerto San Carlos sign about 9 miles after crossing the bridge* over the Rio El Rosario just outside of town. Turn right and try not to go in circles. Do not head out alone as you may need some help digging out or otherwise. And bring that extra can of gas. You can also try driving in from Punta Baja, but the dirt track is very rough and you'll have to go inland from the beach, zig-zagging your way there.

*It is just about where you will get pulled over by the cop who clocked you exceeding the exceedingly slow speed limit over the speed bumps in town. He pulls you over here so you can pay him off away from prying eyes.

Punta San Carlos

Long right point, reefs, offshore reefs and easy inside beachbreak – tons of spread-out surf. Best on souths but breaks on any good swells. Rights and lefts. Heavy winds, but much of it's offshore, making it a great destination for board, kite and windsurfers. Lots of longboarding here, not for mushy surf but because there is a lot of ocean to cover. Tow-ins seem to be catching on here, too. Camping at Punta San Carlos is rough, with no services available, unless you rely n Solo Sports, which is a good bet (see below). And since it's windy the conditions get even more demanding. As mentioned before for this area, bring everything you need, including water. The closest services are hours away in El Rosario. There's a fish camp, so you can get fish, and the tidepooling is good for other seafood delights. But stock up before heading in.

Camping at San Carlos is run by Solo Sports, a windsurfing outfit (www.solosports.net). They charge $5.00 a day for one vehicle and driver, then another $2.50 for each extra person. Kids under 12 are free. In addition, they can supply most of your needs—food, hot showers. Or you can make it easy on yourself and check into their all-inclusive vacation package deals, starting at $1,650/week where they drive you in from San Diego, or there's a fly-in package for $2,250.

To get here from the highway heading south out of El Rosario, look for the Km80 marker and take the dirt track from there. There may be a Punta San Carlos sign, but don't count on it. From here you will probably get lost a bit, but you'll be OK. Plan for at least a two-hour drive. Your destination is basically SSE from the highway, so when in doubt, take the left fork. Don't attempt this drive if without a good truck or 4x4, and be prepared to do your own repairs along the way. This is rough country. If you managed to find your way to Punta San Carlos by taking the dirt tracks from Punta San Antonio or even Punta Baja, the road along the beach ends here, so you must backtrack to Hwy 1 to get to the breaks to the south. Then again, there is so much surf in this stretch between Punta Baja and Punta San Carlos that it makes you wonder why you need to go anywhere else.

Punta Canoas

From the north, this is the first of Baja's famous Seven Sisters, seven right hand point breaks, one right after the other, and all great surf. (This, by the way, is arguable, as some say the Seven Sisters start at Punta Cono.) Canoas is a good right point that faces south and pulls in surf from all directions. There is also a left to surf just to the south. Baja AirVentures used to fly into Canoas as a winter destination, so it's pretty good. They, of course, could do that, but for the rest of us it's a bitch to get there. It's worth it though (or was, read on) because it picks up all swells and stays glassier than other areas. *The Surf Report* says it's sharky, but *all* of Baja is sharky. Leave the highway north of Cataviña and try to use your maps and compass. 4x4 with lots of clearance required. Do not forget the extra gas, water and all supplies. Good luck.

There is a Desert Inn hotel (formerly La Pinta hotel) on the main highway in Cataviña, and gas (sometimes), so if you don't have at least a couple hours of daylight available you might want to settle in for the night here.

Punta Blanca

Right point that breaks on good souths, southwests and wests when they are big enough, and Punta Blanca does need swell. As with all of the Seven Sisters, the surf can be excellent, but again, it needs swell. The point itself is a headland that looks like a small peninsula pointing south, but swells coming from due south to SSE are blocked, so the swells that get in wrap around and hug the point breaking in a northerly direction. The point blocks some of the wind from the west to NW, but the waves wrap to face north, so it's offshore to sideshore. If the surf is small, head north of the point to explore the points, reefs and beach breaks that face west and get more exposure. Way off the beaten path with very tough roads, so again, bring supplies and be prepared. Also, be prepared for some deep sand on the roads, so think twice if you're not prepared to get stuck as this is one of the most remote surf areas of Baja. Head south of here and south swells are increasingly blocked by the Viscaino Peninsula.

Punta Cono

From here on south swells have a more difficult if not impossible time getting in, until you get past Punta Eugenia. Punta Cono is a finger of land pointing southeast. The swells wrap around the point to where they are facing north to northeast when they break, so they point into the afternoon winds, which are onshore on the west side of the point, but offshore where these fast, nearly-perfect rights break. Only breaks on west through northwest swells. If it wasn't mentioned previously, this part of Baja has a lot of wind, and that creates upwelling in the water dropping the ocean temp's substantially. In winter be prepared to use your 4/3, booties and even a hood. It is easiest to get here driving in from the south (more later). The road is difficult, of course, with "moondust" up to your windows, so be sure you have a shovel, time and patience.

Punta Maria

Not to sound like a broken record, but here's another great right point with waves wrapping around the south-pointing land "finger" to the north and into the wind. Needs a good west/northwest to get this right reef/point working, but once it gets going it's great. There is a fish camp and decent camping, so once you get in you can live pretty well. Easiest drive in is to drive north from Punta Santa Rosalillita. More crowded here as the drive in is easier than the points to the north.

El Cardón

Another little right point with the same conditions as the others that's worth checking since the road passes nearby. Better exposed to swells. Airstrip nearby.

Punta Ositos/Punta Lobos

The name depends on who you talk to or which map you use. Either way, it's another good right reef/point. *The Surf Report* warns that it's sharky here, too. That's OK, it's a nice, sandy beach with good camping, although the dirt track leading in can get deep with sand. Needs west/northwest swell.

Punta Negra/Punta Prieta

Again, the name depends on which map you are using. (And don't be confused by the town of the same name [Punta Prieta] on the Transpeninsular Highway.) Nonetheless, it's yet another right reef/point with the same conditions. Needs west/northwest swell. Good camping and a nice, sandy beach. Fairly easy access from Punta Santa Rosalillita from the south.

Punta San Andrés/Tres Alejandros

Great right point with decent camping and funky palapas the locals will rent you for cheap. Best on good west and solid northwest swells. The winter offshores howl through a break in the hills and cliffs that line the beach that funnel right through the campground and into the waves, making the waves hollow and sometimes difficult to catch, and the camping a little rough. (This winter offshore condition holds for much of this area on down to El Tomatal.) But those same winds deposit a lot of sand into the lineup, helping to groom the shape and provide a break from the typical rocky shore. Camping is not bad for the area, with a few structures to block the wind, outhouses and a pretty clear area. This is basically a surfer campsite, with some windsurfers. Cost is the usual $5.00 a day, paid either directly to Alejandro or Peter, his gringo gatekeeper.

To get to Punta (or Puerto, as some maps label it) San Andrés it's best to drive in to Punta Santa Rosalillita first, then head north. It is about five miles to the break. Most of the road into San Andrés is in good shape, but that only lasts up to the mining area, as it's the miners who make sure the road stays good. After that the road turns to a dirt track requiring the high-clearance 4x4.

Punta Santa Rosalillita

Long, perfect, right point that breaks on big, solid wests and northwests. We're too far south now to take in the south swells, but on the bigger northwests and wests this is a great spot to hit. The *Wave-finder Mexico* and some others call this "The Wall." It is not. As regular Baja surfers know, Punta Rosarito is The Wall. This is a "The Wall is too big" option.

Santa Rosalillita was the first of the Escalera Nautica marinas to be built. It never worked, of course, but they still planned to build more of the marinas, finally cancelling the fiasco in 2009. The only good thing to come out of the construction is the great road from the Highway 1.

This dusty fishing village is pretty big for the area, and had been expected to grow with the construction of the marina. The Escalera Nautica's plan included 17,000 hotel rooms (hah!), in the meantime, however, camping will have to do. No problem, campsites are plentiful.

It really doesn't get crowded here, but to get completely away from other surfers, head to the long stretch of Bahía Santa Rosalillita that starts after the little point at the south end of the village. Here you will find reef after reef with no one around for miles, clear blue water and the same grooming offshores. As you approach the north side of Punta Rosarito the waves get bigger as the exposure is now due west so the waves don't have to wrap around. You are now approaching one of the most consistent winter breaks in Baja.

Access to Rosalillita is as easy as it gets. In fact, the access road is paved, and the turnoff from the Transpeninsular is well-marked. (The road itself is wider than the Transpeninsular. Heck, it could be a runway for a 747.) But if you want to head north to the other points of the Seven Sisters you should have a high clearance vehicle, preferably with four-wheel drive. And if you are heading to these breaks in the winter, which is when the best swells are here, you will need to be concerned about rain and the resulting axle-sucking mud. For that, even a 4x4 is insufficient.

Punta Rosarito/The Wall

About 18 miles south of Punta Santa Rosalillita is "The Wall." Consistent, right-breaking reef/point taking in swell from west and northwest. Lefts too, but it's the long rights that put The Wall on the map. There are two main surf areas, but breaks all around depending on swell and tide. Out on the tip of the point is a reef with rights and lefts that's directly exposed to the swell. South of the tip is where the right pointbreaks start, with long walls wrapping around. Unlike the sandy beaches of the Seven Sisters to the north, this beach is all rocks.

There is tons of camping here spread out mostly along the top of the point. Unique to The Wall is the series of bunker-like rock windbreaks built up along the point as campsites—a testament to the windy conditions. Fortunately, those winds are often offshore. Unfortunately, they can howl to the point where it's virtually unsurfable, which also makes hanging out around camp pretty miserable. Nonetheless, The Wall is legendary for its reliability, size, power and good shape. Or legendary for bad conditions. It all depends on when you hit it.

To get to The Wall drive about 400 miles down Mex 1 to the "second" town of Rosarito, this one being quite a bit smaller and less touristy than the Rosarito everyone else knows up by the border. Continue down Mex 1 another five miles or so and look for the Km 61 sign. Just before the sign is an unmarked dirt road heading toward the beach. It is a bit of a rough dirt track, but cars can make it if they stay on the best of the roads. (If not, there's a good chance of a rocks exceeding the car's ground clearance, and that could be bad news. In other words, you want a truck or something with a lot of clearance.) Take this road and in about two miles you will reach the beach where you will head north along the point until you find the surf and campground that suits you. You can also drive in from Punta Santa Rosalillita along the beach. It is a dirt track that's often in pretty good shape, so you can make it in a car, but once again, a high-clearance vehicle is much preferred.

Somewhere around here and heading south the water starts warming up, sometimes getting warmer than Southern California by about five to ten degrees, but that depends on the ferocity and regularity of the winds, too.

El Tomatal/Miller's Landing

Mostly right reef/point breaks, with some lefts here and there. Breaks on wests and northwests. Easy to find the turnoff as there are two good markers. First, there is a real sign. Second, there is a military checkpoint. Once off the highway it gets a little tricky, but be patient. There are two or three areas to surf here, depending on the road conditions (i.e., whether or not you can access them). At the north end of the cove is a little fishing village with cabiñas, Campo Esmeralda, and a right point. (On the other side of Campo Esmeralda there is more right-reef potential, if you are really adventurous.) There are signs that will point the way to Campo Esmeralda, so it's easily found.

El Tomatal proper is a little more difficult to get to, but it's worth it because the waves are a lot better. Start by not following the Campo Esmeralda signs, but instead staying on the best dirt road, passing the white house (1.2 miles) and aiming for the palm tree grove (2.8 miles). Once you pass the palm tree grove you will see a small estuary on your right, a long, windswept sandy beach to the right and in front of you, and a dirt track that seems to disappear into the sand dunes heading off to your left. You can park your vehicle here, or use whatever skills and resources you have to drive through (over) the sand covered dirt track and around the point to the El Tomatal fish camp. There it's, a great right reef/point breaking along a long, cobblestone point. There are also lefts on the north side of the point. The actual Miller's Landing is south of here, but most call El Tomatal Miller's Landing.

Morro Santo Domingo

Anyone heading to Miller's Landing/El Tomatal has seen the point on the map directly to the south. It is sometimes referred to as El Morro, but you will see it on the map as Morro Santo Domingo. And yes, there is surf. Big northwest swells wrap all the way around in towards Laguna Manuela for good, but right point surf, but the swell has to be big. The surf is generally small, make that tiny, but it's a nice sandy beach and the fishing is good, so it's a nice place to camp. Drive in from the main highway rather than try to find your way along the beach from Miller's Landing. Even then, the road can be difficult with deep sand.

Where to Stay Near El Tomatal, Punta Rosarito: Guerrero Negro

Camping is the best option, but you can also drive the hour or more each way to the surf. If that's OK, try the salt-mining, whale-tourism town of Guerrero Negro. Located on the 28th parallel, the border of Baja Sur, Guerrero Negro offers small-town Baja charm, supplies, a bank, medical facilities, and all the comforts for camping-weary surfers (many hotels and restaurants!). It is a bit of a drive to the surf, but it's a break from camping (hot showers!). Plus there is much to do in the area for the non-surfers in your group.

If you are heading straight past Baja Norte for destinations like Abreojos or Cabo, Guerrero Negro makes for a great rest stop. It is about 450 miles below the U.S. border, or roughly a 12-hour drive if there is no traffic.

Lodging Name	Rates	A/C, TV	Credit Cards	Facilities	Comments
Desert Inn Tel. 800-542-3283 (US), 800-026-3605 (Mex) www.desertinns.com	Medium	A/C, TV	Yes	Restaurant Bar	Fomerly La Pinta. Room service. Tours.
Hotel El Morro Tel. 011-52-615-157-0414	Inexpensive	Fans, TV	No	Restaurant Bar	On the west edge of town. Clean and basic. Restaurant opens at 10am.
Hotel Los Caracoles Tel. 011-52-615-157-1088, 011-52-615-161-7518 www.hotelloscaracoles.com.mx	Medium	a/c and fans, TV	Yes	Internet café Wi-fi	Nice place with enclosed courtyard parking. No restaurant, but clean and simple with great service. Tours.
Malarrimo Motel & Trailer Park Tel. 011-52-615-157-0100 www.malarrimo.com	Medium	TV	No	Restaurant Bar Game room Full hook-ups	Best known for its restaurant. Also 22 RV sites—facilities include showers and toilets. Good restaurant and bar. Also known as Cabanas Don Miguelito.

Cedros Island

No really good reports from Cedros, and this writer has never been there. *The Surf Report* speaks of "a few small right points" and Google Earth reveals some surf west of the airport and on the southwest coast. For the hassle getting there, it's worth the time. Then again, there could be awesome surf there that only sailors know about. If you fish, you might consider taking one of the charters out of San Diego to check it.

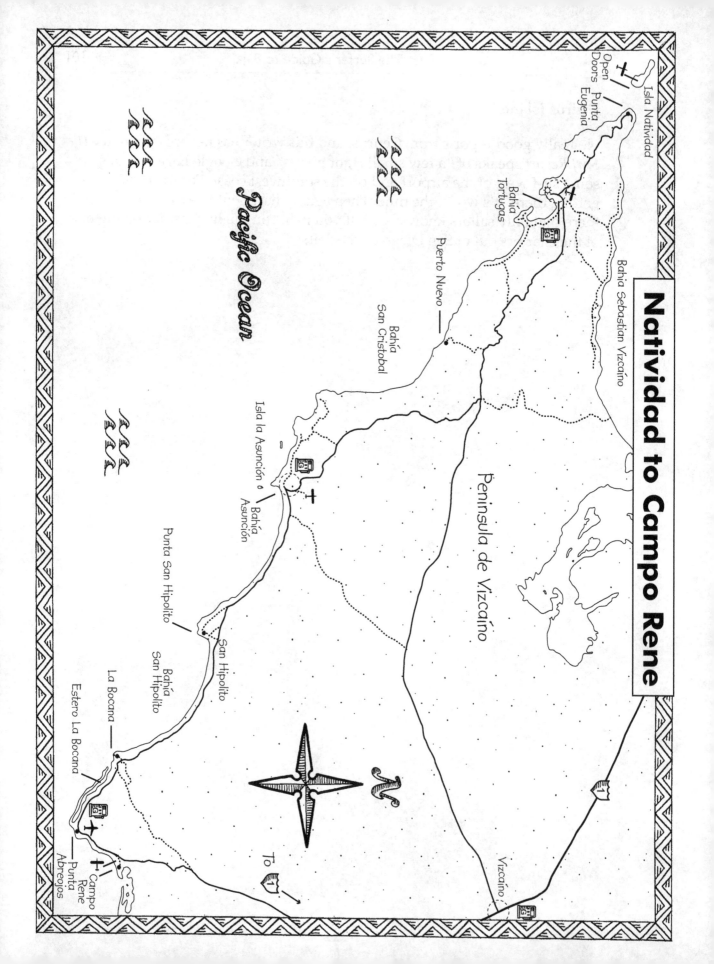

Natividad to Campo Rene

Open Doors

Punta Eugenia

Isla Natividad

Bahía Sebastián Vizcaíno

Bahía Tortugas

Puerto Nuevo

Bahía San Cristobal

Pacific Ocean

Isla la Asunción

Bahía Asunción

Península de Vizcaíno

Punta San Hipolito

Bahía San Hipolito

San Hipolito

La Bocana

Estero La Bocana

Campo Rene

Punta Abreojos

Vizcaíno

To 1

Isla Natividad to Mag Bay

Isla Natividad

One of the best beachbreaks anywhere in the world, with often perfect, hollow grinders. Only breaks on south swells. The waves come in from the south out of deep water and wrap around the east side of the island creating both rights – which are longer, usually better shaped and more frequent – and lefts. This break is the famous **Open Doors**. Gosh, how did they came up with that name? Perhaps the gaping tubes. The sand bottom doesn't explain it. And neither does the short paddle to the line-up.

Unlike most of Baja, the surf doesn't get good until late in the morning, which is when the offshores start. Offshores in the afternoon in Mexico? Yes, it's true. That's because Natividad is close enough to the peninsula to catch the late morning onshores that Baja is famous for, and since this is the east end of the island, the end facing the peninsula, the winds are offshore. So you get offshores from around 10 until sunset. And not only are they offshore, the winds are heated from the dry desert land, which makes the cold water not even noticeable. The other part of all this is that the wind blows onshore in the morning when it's offshore on the peninsula, so dawn patrols are not popular.

Dawn patrols are not needed anyhow, because access to Natividad is difficult, so there are no crowds to beat. To get here you will either need to drive out to Punta Eugenia or Bahía Tortugas and hire a boat, or take the more typical route of flying in with Baja AirVentures. First the latter… Baja AirVentures offers a no-frills, fly-in, fly-out, four-day surf trip. It is sleeping bags, tents or a plywood lean-to, flies, scorpions, dust, seagull shit, and incredible surf. It is on the expensive side (check with them as the price seems to change often), but worth it if you are short on time and long on tube hunger. If you've never flown to a surf destination in a plane big enough for you, your buddy, your boards and the pilot, landed on a dirt strip with hard offshores as a sidewind challenging the surfer-pilot to keep his eyes on trying to keep the plane pointing in the same direction as the landing strip while checking the set wave, and got into the lineup within minutes of taxiing right up to your camp, you haven't lived.

So there is the "luxury" fly-in trip where you go for a few days, or there is the really hard-core Baja surf traveler version where you boat in from Punta Eugenia or Bahía Tortugas. (Actually, real sailors boat in from their last anchorage, which could have been Laguna de Manuela, Cedros or ???.) Punta Eugenia is about 16 miles from Bahía Tortugas and 120 miles from Vizcaíno, 100 of which are unpaved. From either port (Tortugas is a better and more popular marina) you can launch a small boat, assuming you dragged one out here, or hire a panga for about twenty bucks. Natividad is five or six miles out and the boat ride takes about an hour. Best to get the boat in the early morning before the fishermen head out and the wind starts blowing. If you're not bringing camping gear, ask your boat captain if he knows a place to stay, or once you get to the island ask for Chattanooga; he can get you set.

About those tubes.... Here's an idea of just how hollow: On my first trip there I took the Baja AirVentures route. The trip starts on the tarmac at Brown Field outside San Diego where everyone gathers and loads up the plane(s). My buddy Arnold and I were there with our 10-pound limit of gear and surfboards, along with a few other guys we were meeting for the first time. One of the guys had a longboard, which was cool with me, although it didn't seem like the best board choice. My suspicion about board choice was confirmed when the pilot walked up and greeted us as follows:

"Whose board is that?"

"Mine," said the middle-aged weekend warrior.

"Do you know where you are going?" asked the pilot.

In the end the pilot was really just taking advantage of our obvious nervousness. None of us had been there before, and a triple-overhead swell had just peaked, so we were downright scared, and he knew it. As it turned out only one board was broken on the trip—a 7'6" Barry Kanaiapuni pintail, and there was a cut here and there, but no major damage overall. It is a good idea to bring a board for hollow waves with enough heft to get you down the face with hard offshores pushing you out the back. You will not do much turning, or noseriding. In fact, for the most part, the waves are difficult to make. Depending on conditions, you could end up nine of ten unmakeable waves due to the hard offshores and/or shape.

If you go with Baja AirVentures, plan your trip well in advance. Do not wait until you know there is a swell because they are booked way out. The bummer comes when there is no swell as there is *nothing* to do on the island. No bars. No skate park. *Nothing.* And it's hot, windy and dusty. But when there is a solid south swell…

As if Open Doors wasn't enough of a reason to go to Natividad, there are more breaks on the island. **Old Man's** is a comparatively mushy break to the south of Open Doors. Walt Peterson's *The Baja Adventure Book* describes a big-wave winter break on the southwest side of the island in **Siren Bay** that holds. Walt also describes another reef break, **Frijole Bowl**, that breaks off the south end of the island and gets over 20 feet. And supposedly there is another winter big-wave reefbreak off of the northwest point of the island. None of these last three are for beginners. Check with locals or your boat captain for a ride to take you out to these breaks, especially the one on the northwest corner. For the winter breaks, Punta Eugenia may be a better bet as the village on Natividad empties somewhat at that time of year.

Bahía Tortugas (Turtle Bay)

Back on the Vizcaíno Peninsula you will find this big bay with some very occasional and very mediocre surf – heck, make that crappy surf, but you may luck into something at the south end. It's a friendly little town with a couple of hotels making for a surf exploration base camp. It is the most isolated town of reasonable size in all of Baja. Tortugas has restaurants and motels and is also a popular stopping point for traveling yachtspeople. This whole area from Punta Eugenia to Abreojos gets strong afternoon offshores, as the prevailing winds are out of the north ranging from 10 to 30 knots most of the year, calming a bit August through October. The weather changes here, too, with air and water temps getting warmer and even tropical-ish on a very good year. The drive in from Vizcaíno is a little over 100 miles — be sure to fill up with gas — taking four to six hours or even more. It is a washboard rattler that can turn your new Suburban into a bucket-o'-bolts. (If you work on your own vehicle, don't forget to use Loctite liberally before a trip of this sort; make that any Baja trip.) While you should fill up with gas in Vizcaíno, there is a PEMEX gas station here, but they could be out of gas. There is also a paved airstrip next to town. If you have a boat, this is not a bad launch option for Natividad trips, which are about 20 miles from the mouth of this well-protected bay

Where to Stay

There are a couple of friendly, cheap little motels here, so grab a shower and get out of that sleeping bag. While directions can be difficult, especially since no one here speaks any English, finding Motel Nanci is a bit easier as it's the bright blue place on Calle Independecia – hard to miss.

Lodging Name	Rates	A/C	Credit Cards	Facilities	Comments
Motel Nanci Tel. 011-52-615-158-0438, 011-52-615-158-0056	Cheap	No	No	Courtyard parking	Hot shower and a bed!
Motel Rendón Tel. 011-52-615-158-0232	Muy cheap	No	No	Restaurant next door	Hot shower and a bed!

Bahía Asunción (Asuncion Bay)

A big bay with reef breaks out at the point. South swells only. The water gets warmer in these parts, up to 75 degrees or so in the late summer and fall (again, on a good year). If you are driving in from Vizcaíno the turnoff to Asunción is about 45 miles in. This area used to be pretty desolate, but it's perked up in recent years, even having its own website (www.bahiaasuncion.org). It's still not a tourist mecca, but there's an airstrip nearby, a gas station, internet, motel (Hotel El Verduzco) and restaurants. Camping near the town, or anywhere really.

Now for something really interesting. Bahía Asunción has its own surf team, called "Jurjos". While they surf Bahía Asunción, they have another spot they like call Punta Choros. Be nice and they'll show you around.

Punta San Hipolito

South swells pour into fairly good reef breaks around the point. Some beachbreaks, too, but that's not why you head out here. Fairly consistent with south swells. Gets afternoon offshores, like Punta Abreojos. In fact, this is what Surfline calls the "golden zone" of Baja, which is from here to Punta San Juanico. Not sure why, but maybe for the surf?

La Bocana

On some maps it's also marked by the town of La Bocanita. Sand-bottom rights and lefts way out at the mouth of Laguna la Bocana with shape and quality depending on the condition of the sandbar in any given year. Fairly warm water year-round, from the sixties to trunkable. There's also a right that breaks off the reef at the north end of the bay just to the north, La Bocanita. South swells only. Stores, restaurants and gas from the barrel when available in the fishing village. Places to stay include the Baja Bocana B&B (bajabocana@gmail.com) and other guest houses; just ask around. Camping nearby, of course. If Abreojos is your destination, it may be worth taking the 12-mile drive up to check it out. The sand bottom makes for a nice break from the reefs.

Punta Abreojos

Abreojos is Spanish for "open your eyes." And once you see the perfect, hollow rights you will open them wide. The truth is that the early Spanish explorers named this point on account of the reefs here that took their ships, much like they will take your fins on too-small, too-low-tide days. Today, Abreojos is a legendary right point known for perfect rights, football field length rides, hard offshores, and flies the size of seagulls. The offshores make Abreojos popular with the windsurfing set, so along with the fishing fans, you will have some company here, as secluded as it's. Nonetheless, the waves are still fairly uncrowded.

There are a handful of points here, depending on the swell and tide, and they are all found on the east side of the point. The first, biggest easiest is **Burgers**. Then there is **Razors**, the sometimes hairball spot that can break on dry reef. The December 1999 *Surfer* magazine talks about Razors in an article called "Dusted." (Not much written on the spot since as Baja isn't as interesting to the media these days, except when there's some murder involved.) There are also fun beachbreaks found on the south facing beaches around the point to the west (sometimes loaded with stingrays), but most everyone surfs the reefs on the east side.

As mentioned earlier, the reefs are on the east side of the point, much like Natividad, so with the waves breaking to the west the mornings can be slightly onshore, which is slightly offshore everywhere else. In late morning the wind switches offshore—*hard* offshore—and Abreojos comes alive.

Did I mention that the wind blows *hard* offshore? It actually can get hellish. The bummer is that the flies have adapted; they don't blow away, and they swarm in by the zillions, so get ready to do battle. On the positive side, the water can get fairly warm, about 10 degrees warmer than San Diego. But again, those offshores can blow that warm water right off the surface and back out to sea, so bring wetsuits.

Abreojos is easy to find from Highway 1. Just look for the signs and make the turn. The road from Mex 1 into Abreojos is about 50 miles long and is usually in pretty good shape. There's an eatery at the turnoff. You can also fly directly into Abreojos as there is a dirt landing strip nearby. Abreojos is to the west of the airstrip. The guys at Baja AirVentures (see Appendix) may fly you here, reluctantly, or hook it up as part of your Natividad trip (again, reluctantly).

The town of Abreojos has gas and some supplies, and there is pizza and beer at Chelo's, which also has rooms for rent. Supplies, however, are also found at nearby La Bocana or Campo René. There are no hotels to speak of, but you can find rustic lodging at Campo René, about 25 minutes away, or camp pretty much anywhere. The main source of income for the people of Abreojos is the fishing cooperative. So if you fish here remember that is customary to give much of your catch to the cooperative.

Campo René

East of Abreojos up in the bay at Estero de Coyote is Campo René, with reef (about a mile south of the town) and rivermouth breaks. Coming in from Highway 1 you'll reach Campo René before Abreojos. The actual *campo* is on the *estero* side, not facing the ocean. The surf is pretty much all along the beach, from Abreojos to to the estuary. Some good size waves, mostly long lefts, can be found breaking outside the rivermouth, sometimes way outside. (As with all rivermouths, take caution; the currents can be overwhelming.) Along the stretch toward Abreojos there are right points and beachbreaks. As with the rest of the breaks in this part of Baja, it needs a good south. Water stays comparatively warm. The warm water, estuary, and big sandy beach makes the area ripe for stingrays, so be care and do the "shuffle" when walking through the surf.

There's a variety of lodging at Campo René, including campgrounds, RV sites, rustic cabanas (shared facilities) and other makeshift arrangements. Bring a sleeping bag and figure it out.

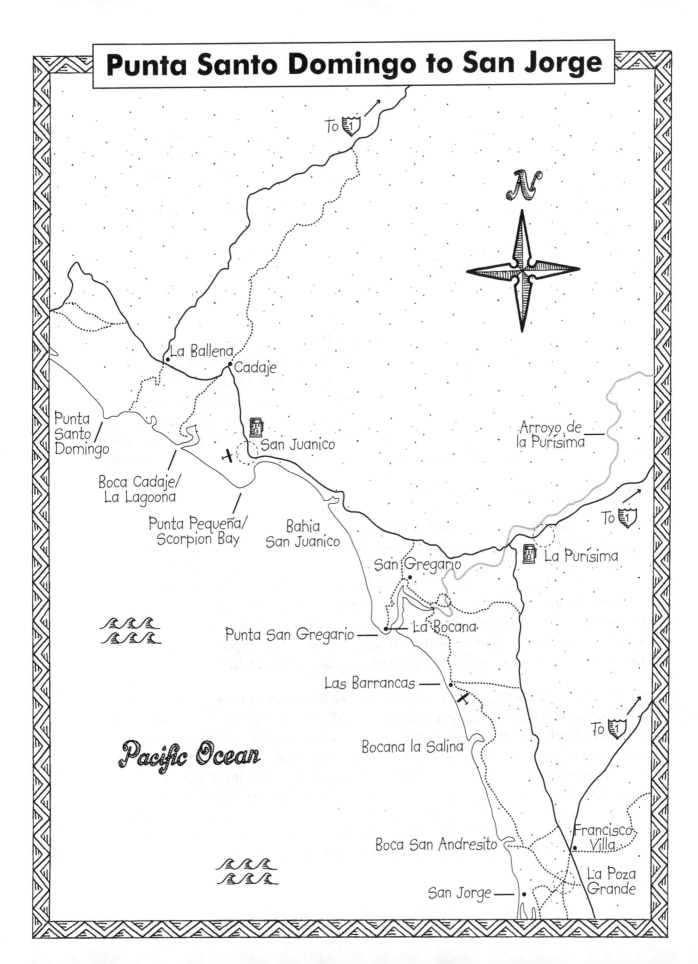

Punta Santo Domingo to San Jorge

To 1

N

La Ballena
Cadaje

Punta
Santo
Domingo

Arroyo de
la Purísima

San Juanico

Boca Cadaje/
La Lagoona

To 1

Punta Pequeña/
Scorpion Bay

Bahia
San Juanico

La Purísima

San Gregario

Punta San Gregario — La Bocana

Las Barrancas —

To 1

Pacific Ocean

Bocana la Salina

Francisco
Villa

Boca San Andresito

La Poza
Grande

San Jorge —

Punta Santo Domingo

Off the beaten track. Needs south swell or a solid west. Waves off the point and beach breaks in the bay. The nearest real town is San Juanico, AKA Scorpion Bay to the south. So what you do is drive out to Cadeja, and follow the road west (left) few miles until reach the arroyo with some structures. This is La Ballena. Turn off onto the road heading SW; it will take you to the point. Check it out when you get bored with Scorpion Bay's crowds; this place is rarely surfed. But you had better be extremely bored, because the drive in is rough, but doable.

La Laguna

There are two rivermouth/estuaries between Punta Santo Domingo and San Juanico. I'm not sure which is the real La Laguna. *Wave-finder Mexico* identifies it as the north estuary, which is Estero San Raymundo. Others point to the estuary to the south and nearer to San Juanico, Boca Cadaje. And don't get it confused with Laguna San Ignacio, where whale watching tours take precedence over surfing. Regardless, it's difficult to get to either one. You can reach Boca Cadaje by taking a dirt track west out the back side of San Juanico.

Bahía San Juanico (Scorpion Bay)

Legendary string of right points starting at the west end of Bahía San Juanico up at Punta Pequeña, a south facing point with a lighthouse. Needs a solid south swell. North swells don't get in and wests need to be big enough to wrap. Altogether there are six different point breaks here, some of which connect depending on the swell. You count the points from the east to west, or more accurately, northeast to southwest. The upper points face more to the west, are sandier and better protected from the winds. The points further out the point are windier and rockier, but catch more west swell.

First point, which is right in front of town, is a nice, sandy beach, but it needs a big south swell to break, so it's usually small, even in summer. Second point is a good beginner spot with an easy, perfectly-shaped, sand-bottom (watch out for stingrays at these sandy beaches) wave on most swells, and turns into a faster and hollower wave on bigger swells. It starts breaking off the rocky point in front of the Scorpion Bay Cantina & Campground. Third point is the source of legends, with rides that connect up Second and First points on big swells. Third gets sketchy on low tides due to the sharp, volcanic rock reef bottom. Lots of guys wear booties. Fourth, Fifth, Sixth and beyond have bigger waves, and get blown out more easily as they are further out the point and more exposed. Up around the point heads to the estuaries mentioned above. Take a look around. You may as well. You drove forever to get here.

Scorpion Bay is a destination unto itself. It is a 14-plus hour drive from the California border, if you drive straight through, so it's best to plan on two days of driving. The easiest route comes up from the south and leaves you with only 30 miles of dirt road to deal with. It is the long way around (Loreto to Ciudad Insurgentes to La Purísima), but kindest on your vehicle and friends. The second least amount of off-roading has you coming in from the east for about 60 miles of dirt road (Mulege to Rosarito to La Purísima). It is more direct, cutting about 200 miles off of your total drive from Tijuana, but you should have a four-wheel drive vehicle or truck, and mud and flash floods are frequent hazards when it rains. If you really like off-road driving you can come in from the north road and create about 105 miles and five hours of dust clouds. Take the turnoff toward Abreojos at San Angel (before reaching San Ignacio), go left (southeast) to El Alamo, then right (southwest) toward the Fridera Fish Camp. From the lagoon head south to Cuarenta then on to San Juanico. This north route is for the truly hardcore off-roader. It is easy to get lost and find yourself where no one comes around for days or maybe weeks. Basically, you have to love off-roading and be well-prepared. You also might want to check the forums at www.scorpionbay.net for road conditions in advance.

The dirt roads leading in are graded periodically, but don't expect them to have been prepared for your arrival. If you end up driving in at night – a ridiculous idea – look out for livestock on those dirt roads. Good luck.

There is another option that cuts travel time to one day: Fly/drive. Fly into Loreto or La Paz and rent a Jeep or pick-up. The drive from either is under four hours.

The Scorpion Bay area including the town of San Juanico has grown, with surfers, campers, fishermen and tourists coming from all over the world. The popularity means commerce, so the town of San Juanico has ample provisions, including a PEMEX station. (There is another station back in Mulege.) As popular as Scorpion Bay has become, however, there is little lodging other than the palapas at the Scorpion Bay Resort, a few homes available to rent, and now the Scorpion Bay Surfing & Fishing Club, a resort of sorts.

Scorpion Bay Resort (scorpionbay.net): Great place. Palapas, camping, a good restaurant and cantina. Internet access, too. The RV sites are just off the beach. Camping costs 150 pesos per person per day, but kids under seven are free. Palapas go for 300 pesos per day for one or two persons, 100 pesos per extra person. They fit up to eight and come with cots, sleeping bags and a semi-private bath with hot shower. Email ahead to reserve (ruben@scorpionbay.net) or call (619-239-1335 US, or 011-52-613-138-2850).

Scorpion Bay Club (scorpionbayclub.com): Private club with very nice houses and casitas. Prices range from $91/night to $228, unless you're an owner or a guest of an owner, then the prices are lower. All the amenities you could want, but it's not a hotel. Think condo, but meals and other hotel-like amenities can be arranged. Head to their Facebook page for surf reports (facebook.com/scorpionbayclub).

As mentioned, some of the houses that have recently been built are available to rent, ranging from basic rentals up to over $300/night. Find yours online.

By the way, be sure to check on the running of the Baja 1000 before heading down. It usually runs in November, and San Juanico is one of the stops.

Punta San Gregorio

If you follow the beach from Scorpion Bay south to the next point you will find a reef and a rivermouth/pointbreak, both catching a good bit of swell – more than Scorpion Bay. So when Scorpion is not big enough or if the swell is coming more out of the west, heading south is an option. Sometimes the rights wrap into the estuary/rivermouth (Boca San Gregorio) and break facing north, so the winds are offshore. Driving out of Scorpion Bay towards La Purisma the turnoff is at about the 20 mile marker.

Las Barrancas

Southwest facing beaches with offshore reefbreaks taking wests to strong souths (that get past Cabo San Lazaro). Lefts and rights. Small town fronts the breaks. Signs from highway 53 mark the turn.

San Andresito

Rivermouth to the north and a reef/point facing southwest picking up west to southwest swells. Way off the grid. No one goes here except the fishermen.

Some good surf, but not the best winds. Take the dirt track from the 53 south to Poza Grande, then head northwest followed by a bend to the west.

San Jorge

Beachbreaks with similar swell direction needs as Las Barrancas and Andresito. Not marked well on many maps, the San Jorge fish camp is found southwest of La Poza Grande at the northwest part of the estuary. As a surf spot, San Jorge really refers to the beachbreaks all along the estuaries and barrier peninsula south of San Andresito also known as Bocanita San Rafael and Boca las Animas. Practically speaking, you should leave this area to boat exploration.

Isla Magdalena, Punta San Lazaro, Punta Hughes, Magdalena or Mag Bay

Rocky point breaks catching souths and big wests on Isla Magdalena. Good offshores at the right breaks. It is not easy to get here. If you are looking for even more adventure and seclusion than you will find in most of Baja, head to Puerto San Carlos and find a boat to either take you to Puerto Magdalena, where you'll need to get a ride out to the surf, or arrange for the boat captain to take you straight to the surf. There's nothing on this arid island, except the little town of Puerto Magdalena (no electricity or running water), so bring everything you need. If you are smart, however, you will just hook up with Mag Bay Tours (magbaytours.com). They are the Mag Bay experts and have been doing this for years. They also do sportfishing and whale watching tours, so they know the area inside out. Practically speaking, it's the only reasonable way to surf Isla Magdalena. So if you're looking for a boat captain or someone to get you out there, just ask around for Steve Warren, the guy who owns Mag Bay Tours.

For the Mag Bay Tours trip you will need to fly into Loreto, where you will catch a 2½-hour van ride to Puerto San Carlos in Bahía Magdalena. The next morning they will ferry you out to Puerto Magdalena and truck you on to one of the base camps (which one depends on the surf) located on Isla Magdalena. Unlike some surf-tour serviced destinations, you will not have to worry about crowds. The only surfers here are with the tour, which is limited to 12 people. The camp itself has large, double-occupancy standup dome tents, each with its own shaded and wind protected porch. The cost (as of this writing) runs $1,360 for eight days (six full surf days) plus your airfare to Loreto. You can also arrange trips of shorter or longer lengths. Plan and book way in advance.

The island gets surf from the north and south, and Mag Bay Tours used to move its camp with the seasons, but now it focuses on the south swells, opening May through October.

The surf camp is right over the island's best surf, three right-hand points—**Cuevas**, **Campsites** and **Bathtubs**—catching southern hemi's and hurricane swells with nice offshores prevailing. Cuevas is most consistent and handles any size swell. The breaks are inside the point at the north end of the big bay, Bahia Santa Maria. That point is Punta Hughes, AKA Punta San Lazaro. The waves wrap around the point up into the wind for good offshores. Mostly easy waves with good shape, if a bit slow, depending on the size. When it gets big, well, it's not as easy. It's rocky, with lava rocks, not cobblestones, and that makes some nervous. Just don't go straight.

Where to Stay

If you're not staying with Mag Bay Tours on the island, or camping, there are two hotels in Puerto San Carlos. The primarily cater to whale watching tourists and sport fishermen, but surfers are not strangers here.

Lodging Name	Rates	A/C, TV	Credit Cards	Facilities	Comments
Hotel Alcatraz Tel. 011-52-613-136-0017	Moderate	Yes, no	No	Restaurant Bar	Family owned and run.
Hotel Brennan Tel. 800-831-9041 (US), 011-52-(613)13-602-88 Hotelbrennan.com.mx	Moderate	Yes, Fans	No	Wi-fi	Whale and sportfishing tours.

PUNTA CONEJO TO MIGRIÑO

Between Mag Bay and Punta Conejo are miles of islands, like Isla Santa Margarita and Isla Cresciente, and rivermouths like Boca Guadalupe, with surf yet to be discovered, or more accurately, discussed. Without a boat, or a boatload of time and resourcefulness, the next stop south is Punta Conejo. But if you have an yearning for discovery and adventure, here it's. Especially if you are a goofy foot, as there are some lefts…

Mexico 1 bends toward the west coast near Punta Conejo, so if you've been driving down the 1 this is a good place to get off the highway and back to the beach. From Punta Conejo to the end of the peninsula you'll find relatively easy beach access and year-round surf. As you near Cabo it gets more crowded.

Punta Conejo

When the swell gets big head to Punta Conejo. It can handle it, even if you can't. Punta Conejo is a point formed by thousands of years of arroyo runoff, with long, excellent lefts and some rights. The point juts out WSW so it catches nearly all swells. (So you don't have to wait for it to get big.) Gets especially windy during the summer, but this is when the waves are best. Buy oysters by the dozen from the commercial divers; lobsters too. Camping in the dunes and all along the beach. The dirt road along the beach offers many surf opportunities to the south and north, with totally uncrowded points, reefs and beachbreaks. Coming from the north the turnoff to Punta Conejo is about 14 miles out of El Cien, which is a good place to fill up on gas. The turnoff isn't marked. The offroad driving is manageable without four wheel drive. There's always a crew camping out here, so you don't have to worry about being alone (if that's a concern).

Punta Marquez

Lots of rock reefs all around this area near El Cedro. Punta Marquez faces southwest, but catches swells from all directions. Not crowded, but the waves aren't as good as other nearby spots, like Punta Conejo to the north. Camping only. It gets windy here, especially in the summer, and as with Conejo, these aren't "good" winds, so Marquez is also a popular destination for kite and wind surfing. If you're coming in from Punta Conjeo it's basically a straight run down the road that parallels the coast. This area is La Ballena Preserve and there's surf all along here with no one out. Turn west at the little compound. From Highway 1 turn at the bus stop just south of the km56 marker. There should also be a green *Conquista Agraria* sign. Bear to the right at the fork; don't head towards *Ejido Conquista Agraria*. Well, you can, and you'll reach the beach at other breaks just south of Punta Marquz. The drive is much shorter from Punta Conejo. From Punta Marquez south are miles and miles of uncrowded white-sand beaches and surf, and for the first 10 miles the (dirt) road can be pretty good. Along the way you'll cross a couple of arroyos/rivermouths, like La Bocana.

La Bocana

There are a bunch of arroyos and dry rivermouths along the stretch from Punta Marquez to La Pastora. (I know, that describes most of Baja.) There is a particularly large arroyo near Los Inocentes that doesn't often breach the ocean but still has water, often called La Bocana (not to be confused with the La Bocana in Cabo). Anyhow, there are sandbars and waves here, and the road into Los Inocentes can be pretty good. Camp anywhere along this stretch. But as with all arroyos and rivermouths, be careful during rainy season for flash flooding.

La Pastora

The Cabo-area locals consider this their big-wave spot. Surf shops proudly feature photos of the double- and triple-overhead rights. La Pastora is a long sandy beach about five miles north of Todos Santos with rights and lefts, but is best known for the big rights that break with winter northwest swells. It also takes in summer southern swells. Always bigger than most other nearby spots. Better on mid to lower tides. *The Surf Report* describes it as a point, but it's really more like a bend in the coast combined with an arroyo. To get there, take the road (Calle Topete) northwest out of Todos Santos that heads past the Todos Santos Inn. As you head out of town the road drops down a little hill into a green shaded area. When you crest the other side turn left, or toward the beach. The turnoff is about six kilometers from there. To find the turnoff (another challenge) stay on the road as it passes out of the town to the northwest. As you crest the hill just out of town you can see the sand point with waves breaking in the distance. Now look for the clump of palm trees; it's a coco palm farm. Just on the other side of the palm grove is a horse corral followed by a left turnoff onto a dirt road. That road takes you straight to the beach. The sandy point is to the north out in front of the palapa with the low wall on the beach. The lefts are a little further north. Do not get stuck in the sand. As with this whole southwest coast, winds can be a problem, with the onshores starting late morning.

You can stay in Todos Santos and drive in and out, or look online for a casita rental and walk to La Pastora. Find rentals at Casitasurf.com, Calycanto.com, VRBO.com and more.

Todos Santos

Gas up. Shower up. Sleep in a bed. Wi-fi. People watch at a cafe. If you've been driving in from the north, surfing and camping, you're back in civilization.

This Todos Santos is not to be confused with the big wave island off of Ensenada. And it's definitely not to be confused with the party town to the south, Cabo San Lucas. This Todos Santos is billed as an artist settlement turned tourist destination. Everything is here—nice hotels, restaurants, great fish taco and ceviche stands, camping, gas, repairs, and other benefits, so it's a decent place to hang. And there is surf just outside town, much of it to the south. As with most spots in this area, the best quality surf comes in the winter with northwest and west swells, but it works just fine with summer south swells, too.

Getting to the surf south of town is easy; the main road takes you right out to Hwy 19 south. Finding your way to the surf north of town is a little more difficult. (See La Pastora above.)

Get good information on the town of Todos Santos and the surrounding area at www.todossantos-baja.com. The locals take September off, so many of the restaurants and other businesses are closed then.

Where to Stay in Todos Santos

Lodging Name	Rates	A/C /TVs	Credit Cards	Facilities	Comments
Casa Bentley Tel. 011-52-612-145-0276 www.casabentleybaja.com	Moderate to expensive	Yes	No	Pool Wi-fi	Outdoor kitchen for group meals. Laundry services. Tours.

El Molino Trailer Park Tel. 800-966-7420 (US), 011-52-612-124-0140	Cheap	No	No	Restaurant Bar RV hookups Pool	At the south end of town behind the PEMEX. Toilets, showers, laundry. 21 sites. Been here 25 years.
Hostería Las Casitas Tel. 011-52-612-145-0255	Moderate	No	No	Restaurant Camping	Bed and breakfast with some shared baths. Rate includes breakfast.
Hotel California Tel. 011-52-612-145-0525 www.hotelcaliforniabaja.com	Expensive	Fans	Yes	Restaurant Bar Pool Wi-fi	As in Don Henley? Legendary hotel in the heart of the historical district. Nice place for couples. Has room service, a rarity.
Hotel Guluarte Tel. 011-52-612-145-0006	Cheap	A/C or fans	No	Pool Laundry	The sign says "Hotel-Supermercado Y Lavanderia", which means they have a market and laundramat. A/C costs extra.
Hotel Miramar Tel. 011-52-612-145-0341	Cheap	No	No	Restaurant Pool Laundry	Some ocean views from upstairs. A bit away from town center, but you can walk to Punta Lobos. Pets allowed.
Maria Bonita Hotel Tel. 011-52-612-145-0850	Moderate	Yes, yes	Yes	Restaurant	Located in the center of town. A/C costs extra.
Hotel Santa Rosa de las Palmas Tel. 011-52-612-145-0394	Moderate	Yes, yes	No	Pool Jacuzzi Parking Wi-fi	Kitchenettes and living rooms
Posada La Poza Tel. 011-52-612-145-0400 www.lapoza.com	Muy Expensive	A/C, no TVs	Yes	Restaurant Bar Pool Wi-fi	Swiss owners. No kids under 12 allowed. Ocean views. Upscale boutique hotel just outside town center on the estuary next to the beach. Great for weddings. Look for the signs that say "La Poza."
Todos Santos Inn Tel. 011-52-612-145-0040 www.todossantosinn.com	Expensive	Some A/C, no TVs	Yes	Restaurant Bar Wine bar	Solitude, peace and quiet in an historic, elegant setting right in town. No TVs, radios or telephones—a good thing here. Closed in September. Book in advance as there are only 8 rooms.

Punta Lobos

Also called Todos Santos. Pangas and pelicans, but not great surf. Breaks on south swells. Closest break to Todos Santos, found south of town at Km 54, then west 1.5 miles to the beach. Points and reefs, but the main wave is the left that occasionally breaks around the point/headland. If you have been driving south you will have noticed that the lineups are now starting to get a bit crowded – at least as compared to the breaks further north. That's also a sign that you need to beware of thievery, which is the case for the whole area.

Punta Conejo to Migriño

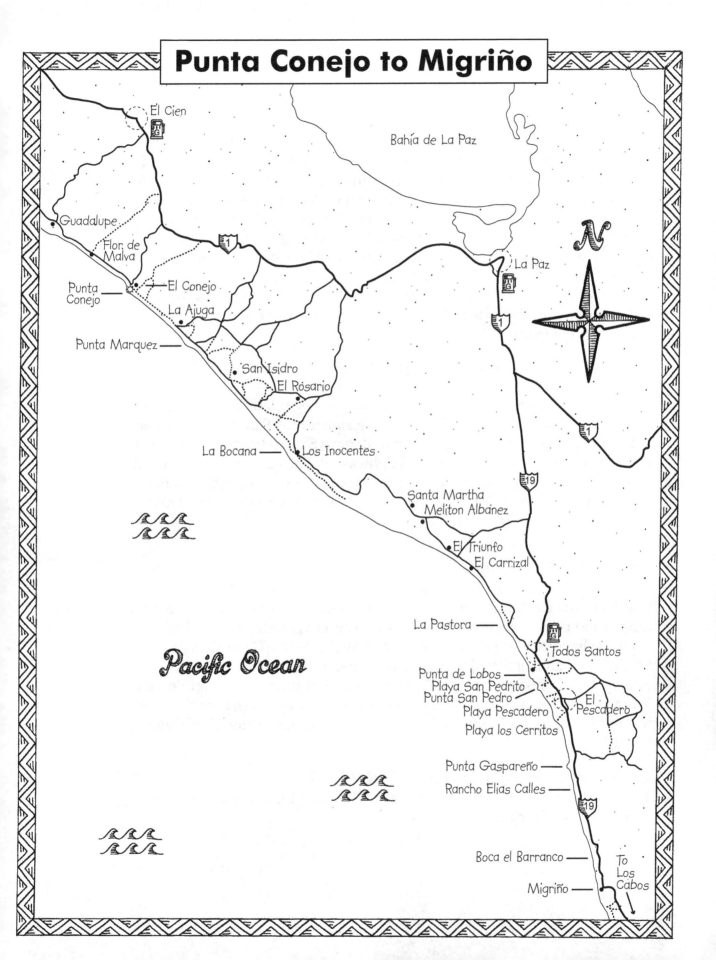

Playa San Pedrito

About 6 kilometers south of Todos Santos and just north of the Km59 marker is the turnoff for Playa San Pedrito, aka Palm Beach, La Playa Palmas, or El Estero (as the locals call it). You can also turn at Km57 across from the *Jardin Botanico Campo Experimental* (head south then west). The beach itself is less than 3 kilometers from the turnoff. Good beachbreak breaking on most swells, but best on west and northwest swells, with rights and lefts, and hollow lefts peel off the south point on south swells. This is a great little beach nestled in a coconut palm grove giving it a bit of a tropical feel, a pleasant change from the typical desert conditions of Baja. And it's spitting distance from the comforts of Todos Santos. There are often campers here, so you'll have company.

Pescadero, Punta San Pedro, Playa San Pedro

Just south of Playa San Pedrito or about four miles south of Todos Santos at the Km59 marker is the turnoff with the big sign for the San Pedrito RV Park (now closed), which is where you will find Playa San Pedro, better known as Pescadero, after the nearby town on Highway 19. The beach is cobblestoned at the north end and transitions to sand as you go south. The cobblestoned beach is also known as San Pedro, as it's closest to Punta San Pedro. This whole stretch picks up all swells nicely.

Where to Stay for Pescadero

Check out the Pescadero Surf Camp (www.pescaderosurf.com). They have a cabaña and private palapa camping with electricity, lights, and full bathroom. Each site handles four people. Tent rentals available too. Campsites are $10/day; cabaña for $40/day plus $5 per person. They also offer board rentals, surfing lessons and surf "safaris," and they carry some supplies, too. You will find the camp just off the east side of Highway 19 (not on the beach) just north of Cerritos at Km-64. Look for the rock sign reading "Surf Camp Pescadero."

Closer to the beach is the San Pedrito Surf Hotel (www.sanpedritosurf.com). The casitas have kitchenettes, there's a restaurant, wi-fi, and you're right there at the surf breaks.

There used to be an RV park here, San Pedrito RV Park (yes, the San Pedrito beach is the next cove to the north), but it went away with a hurricane.

Lodging Name	Rates	A/C	Credit Cards	Facilities	Comments
Pescadero Surf Camp Tel. 011-52-612-134-0480 www.pescaderosurf.com	Muy cheap to moderate	No	Yes	Pool Camping	Cabañas to campsites. Surf camp with board rentals, tours and lessons. Guided surf safaris take you to the best surf for you. Located at Km64 just off Hwy 19.
San Pedrito Surf Hotel Tel. 001-52-1-612-133-9602 www.sanpedritosurf.com	Moderate	Yes, No	Only for deposits	Restaurant Bar Billiards Laundry Wi-fi	7 cool casitas right at the beach in front of the surf. Kitchenettes in rooms with utensils and other items. Room safes.

Playa Los Cerritos

Cerritos has become quite a scene over the years, especially for beginner surfers. It's transformed from a wide open camping beach to homes, condos, surf shops, showers and a beach club. That's OK; the waves are still there, and you can still camp. Cerritos is primarily a right reef/point with great beachbreaks breaking best on winter northwest swells, and of course it picks up souths too. The sandy beach is long with lots of peaks. It's probably the most crowded spot on the West Cape due to its consistency, shape, accessibility and party atmosphere. Cerritos faces southwest and is a bit blocked by the point at the north end. It's a fairly good beach for beginners, except when it gets big, of course. Wind blows onshore in the afternoons, as it does in this whole area. There are two board rental shops on the beach, the Costa Azul Surf Shop and El Diablo Blanco, and there's a (pricey) restaurant and bar on the sand called Cerritos Beach Club. A nice place to hang between surfs. Directions: Head south out of Todos Santos on Hwy 19 about 12 kilometers to about 1 kilometer after the Km-64 marker.

Where to Stay at Playa Los Cerritos

Lodging Name	Rates	A/C /TVs	Credit Cards	Facilities	Comments
Cerritos Surf Colony Tel. 971-544-7645, 503-781-8954 www.cerritossurfcolony.com	Muy Expensive to muy muy expensive	Yes/ no	Yes	Pool BBQ Wi-fi	On the beach, expensive condo rentals. Kitchenettes. Very nice, if you can afford it.

Hacienda Cerritos Tel. 971-544-7645, 503-781-8954 www.haciendacerritos.com	Muy, muy, muy expensive	Yes/no	Yes	Pools Wi-fi	Walk to surf. Lord over Playa Los Cerritos. This is the mansion on the hill over the point. Run by the same people as Cerritos Surf Colony. Private pools, kitchens, fireplaces, helicopter services…you know, the usual stuff.

Punta Gaspareño

If you walked a few miles down the beach from Playa Los Cerritos you would come to a steep, lava rock headland with surf on the south side. Or find the turnoffs from Highway 19 at around Km73. Coming from the north look for the turnoff near the top of the hill at the headland in the S-curve; from the south the turnoffs are easily seen, as is the surf, because the Highway 19 is close to the beach here. There's surf in the protected lee of the rocky headland (on smaller swells) and more open beach breaks as you head south. As with much of this area, Punta Gaspareño breaks best on bigger wests and northwest swells, and blows out late morning, but the headland can protect it a bit from north winds – except when it's big and the waves break further out, and then a right starts showing off the point. It's never crowded here, especially close to the point. Don't confuse Punta Gaspareño with the village on the map to the south, El Gaspareño.

Plutarco Elías Calles/Boca de San Jacinto

From Punta Gaspareño you can look south and see Plutarco Elias Calles/Boca de San Jacinto, but you probably won't notice it. The same is true from the highway. No one ever heard of Elías Calles until after 2000, and now it's in every surf guide and map. This rivermouth sand point (arroyo) with cobblestone bottom picks up any south, southwest or west swells, but the best shape is from the souths. Juicy and often hollow, with better lefts than the rights.

To reach Elías Calles turn off the highway arount Km78 at the San Jacinto riverbed/arroyo. It is really wide with a nice bridge so you can't miss it. It is the biggest riverbed in the area. If you have eagle eyes you can look for the pink house on the beach side of Highway 19 with the Mini Super Delia. It's just south of the arroyo at Km79 and there's an easy road to the beach. Or just find your way into the riverbed if your vehicle can handle the sand (dry season only). You can also stay at the namesake bed and breakfast, Rancho Elías Calles which is right in front of the surf break.

Where to Stay for Rancho Elías Calles

Lodging Name	Rates	A/C	Credit Cards	Facilities	Comments
Rancho Elías Calles Cell 011-52-612-152-2369 (but don't depend on it) Email: rancheoeliascalles @yahoo.com	$65 per person, meals included, can rent without	No	Cash only	Private patio dining Direct TV Ping Pong	Either full meal plan or just rent a room. Right in front of the surf. Your host Roger is a real character. Originally from SoCal, Roger's a long-time Baja resident who knows the surf in this area probably better than the fish.

Migriño

Long stretch of ordinary beachbreak catching lots of swell. This whole stretch has become a giant ATV/quad playground. There are better places to surf and hang out. The Rancho Migriño turnoff is about 26 kilometers from Cabo San Lucas

Cabo San Lucas to the East Cape

Cabo is California's favorite escape from the cold of winter. The difference between a 4/3 and trunks is just a two-hour flight from Los Angeles. Facing southwest to southeast, Cabo picks up surf from all directions in all seasons.

The Cabo "Corridor" is the most luxurious stretch of Baja, featuring some of the most expensive upscale resorts in the world. For surfers who have been traveling the length of Baja for decades, this Baja is at once shocking and disappointing. The growth of upscale/high-rise hotels and condos is shocking. The reduced access and lack of wide-open spaces for camping is disappointing. But for most, it's not all bad. And the good news is that it gets better as you head east.

Cabo's beautiful beaches, emerald blue water and dry climate appeal to sun worshippers worldwide, often putting the squeeze on surfers who just want a wave. But if you are looking for a surf trip your non-surfing friends or family will enjoy, or anyone looking for comfort, upscale accommodations, world-class partying, or all three—then this is the place. And for golfers there are at least six top-notch golf courses here, but you golfers already know that. Tourist season peaks from November through March or Spring Break, as do the prices. Hotel room rates start dropping around May, which is also an awesome month for the south swells that light up this coast, and air fares drop considerably in July. So as the prices drop the surf picks up, and that's just how we like it.

As mentioned, public beach access continues to decline due to private development, even though it's illegal for anyone to completely block access to any beach in Mexico. Public access to the beach is often marked with blue and white signs along the highway labeled "Acceso a Playa." Fortunately, or unfortunately, depending on your wallet, precious few of the hotels are right in front of the breaks, so expect to drive to the surf.

Where to Stay for Cabo San Lucas and San José del Cabo

There are a zillion places to stay between Cabo San Lucas and San José del Cabo, and the number is going up all the time. The best-known hotels are very expensive – way too expensive for most surfers, but some of them are listed here anyhow. There is also a bunch of moderate and cheap hotels, as well as a few RV parks. Or you can subsidize another surfer's vacation condo by renting it by the day, week or even month, and save yourself some restaurant bills. In the high season (November to May), you will probably need to reserve your place well in advance. In the off season you can head down without a reservation and negotiate pretty good deals at the front desk—something that's more difficult to do over the telephone or Internet.

While there are a zillion places to stay, you will also have to decide whether you want to be closer to the East Cape, West Cape, or right on top of the breaks in the Corridor itself. Then there is the world-famous party scene of Cabo San Lucas to consider. If you stay in Cabo San Lucas, you can enjoy the party craziness without risking your life driving back to your hotel or condo. You are also centrally located for the West Cape and the Corridor. The East Cape, however, is about a 90-minute drive away, for at least three hours of driving on party nights. San José del Cabo is centrally located for the East Cape and the Corridor and is much quieter if you want to avoid the craziness of Cabo San Lucas. Check ahead for the surf forecast. If there are no south swells and only northwest swells, stay in Cabo or the west coast.

Lodging Name	Rates	A/C, TV	Credit Cards	Facilities	Comments
Best Western Hotel & Suites Las Palmas Tel. 866-539-0036 www.bestwestern.com	Expensive	All, Satellite TVs	Yes	Restaurant Pool Wi-fi	San José del Cabo. Kitchens, in-room phones, room service. Not near the beach. Good for airport proximity.
Cabo Inn Tel. 619-819-2727 (US), 011-52-624-143-0819 www.caboinnhotel.com	Moderate	All, No	No	Pool Communal kitchen	Centrally located in Cabo San Lucas. Small rooms, but not a bad place for the price and being in town. TV in common area.
Cabo Surf Hotel Tel. 858-964-5117 (US), 011-52-624-142-2666 www.cabosurfhotel.com/en	Expensive to muy expensive	A/C, Satellite TV	Yes	Restaurant Bar Pool Jacuzzi Surf shop Board rentals Wi-fi	San José del Cabo. Km.28. Right over Acapulquito. Kitchens, patios, continental breakfast included. All rooms are oceanfront with two double-beds. Surf shop on the premises. Legend Mike Doyle gives surf instruction. Kind of a crowded scene. And noisy at night due to the trucks on the highway.

Casa Natalia Tel. 888-277-3814 (US), 011-52-624-146-7100 www.casanatalia.com	Muy expensive	A/C, Satellite TVs	Yes	Restaurant Bar Pool Wi-fi	Nice boutique hotel in San José del Cabo. Phones and everything else in rooms. Smaller and more private than most others. Some jacuzzi suites. No kids. The beach is a bit of a walk away, but there is a shuttle.
Casa Terracotta Bed & Breakfast Tel. 011-52-624-142-4250	Moderate to expensive	Fans	No	Kitchen Laundry	Quaint, simple 4-casita B&B across the highway from Zippers with a good view of the surf. Rate includes a great breakfast.
Club Cabo Motel & Campground Resort Tel. 562-259-7986 (US), 011-52-624-143-3348 mexonline.com/clubcabo.htm	Moderate	A/C, TVs	No	Pool Jacuzzi RV hookups Laundry Wifi	Cabo San Lucas. Walk to Playa Medano. Interesting place. An RV park with air-conditioned suites with kitchens and tent camping. Pet friendly.
El Arco Trailer Park Tel. 011-52-624-143-0613	Inexpensive			Restaurant Pool RV hookups	Three miles east of Cabo San Lucas across the highway from Monuments. RV park with camping, full facilities and hookups.
El Delfin Blanco Tel. 011-52-624-142-1212 www.eldelfinblanco.net	Moderate+	Some, no TVs	Yes	BBQ Wifi	Less than 2 miles east of San José del Cabo on the road to the East Cape in a fishing village. Close to town but quiet. Refrigerators in rooms.
El Encanto Inn Hotel & Suites Tel. 011-52-624-142-0388 www.elencantosuites.com	Moderate-expensive	All, Satellite TVs	Yes	Pool Room service from local restaurants	In the San José del Cabo art district.
Holiday Inn Resort Los Cabos (formerly Presidente Los Cabos) Tel. 800-327-0200 (US), 011-52-624-142-0211; www.ichotelsgroup.com/HolidayInn	Muy expensive	All, TVs	Yes	Restaurants Bar Pool Jacuzzis Fitness spa Tennis Playground	San José del Cabo. All-inclusive (meals, drinks). Short walk to Estero/La Bocana. Good for kids. Hey, it's a Holiday Inn!
Hotel Colli Tel. 011-52-624-142-0725 www.hotelcolli.com	Moderate	A/C, Cable TV	No	Parking garage Wifi	San José del Cabo. Good, clean, in-town location.
Hotel Diana Tel. 011-52-624-142-0490	Cheap	Yes, TVs	No		Clean and basica in downtown San José del Cabo on the plaza. No windows in the rooms, but maybe that makes you feel safer.
Hotel Palmilla Tel. 866-829-2977 (US), 011-52-624-146-7000 palmilla.oneandonlyresorts.com	MUY expensive	A/C, TVs	Yes	Restaurants Bars Pools Golf Gym Tennis Volleyball Wifi	On the point with its namesake break. This is top shelf all the way. Sportfishing, scuba, etc. And a free oxygen shot with every stay.

Hotel Posada Señor Mañana Tel. 011-52-624-142-1372 www.srmanana.com	Inexpensive	Some A/C	No	Pool Communal kitchen Wifi	San José del Cabo. A budget surfer favorite. Nothing fancy, and a bit quirky. Includes continental breakfast. Some rooms have refrigerators and cable TV. 25 minute walk to surf (Estero).
Hotel Posada Terranova Tel. 011-52-624-142-0534 www.hterranova.com.mx	Moderate	A/C, Satellite TVs	Yes	Restaurant Bar	Downtown San José del Cabo near everything. Room service.
Hotel Santa Fe Tel. 011-52-624-143-4401,2,3	Moderate	A/C, TVs	Yes	Pool Store Wifi	Cabo San Lucas near Medano Beach. This one is not the Riu Santa Fe. Clean and quiet. Kitchenettes. Room service.
La Fonda del Mar B&B Tel. 011-52-624-145-2139 www.buzzardsbar.com	Moderate	Fans	No	Restaurant Bar Wifi	Better known as Buzzards Bar & Grill. B&B East of San José del Cabo on the beach on the way to Shipwrecks and the rest of the East Cape. Includes breakfast. Private and shared showers. Fishing charters.
La Jolla de Los Cabos Condos Tel. 800-455-CABO (US), 011-52-624-142-3000	Expensive	A/C, TVs	No	Restaurant Bar Pools Gym	Condo rentals near San José del Cabo and Zippers. Full kitchens.
La Playita Resort Tel. 888-242-4166 (US), 626-962-2805 (US), 011-52-624-24166 www.laplayitahotel.com	Moderate	A/C, Satellite TVs	Yes	Restaurant Bar Pool	San José del Cabo. Not really a "resort," but a nice hideaway on the beach outside town on the way to the East Cape breaks. Great seafood restaurant. Two penthouses with kitchenettes.
Las Misiones de San José Tel. 907-373-3874 (US), 011-52-624-142-1401 Email: condo@matnet.com	Expensive	A/C, TVs	No	Restaurant Bar Poolside grill Pools Tennis Golf	Condo rentals in San José del Cabo. Nice, fully equipped, upscale condos are a pretty good deal. Rates drop April through September. Do not confuse with the hotel overlooking Monuments.
Las Ventanas al Paraíso Tel. 888-767-3966 (US), 011-52-624-144-2800 www.lasventanas.com	MUY expensive	A/C, Cable	Yes	Restaurant Bar Pool Fitness center Spa Wifi	Cabo San Lucas at Km 19.5. Short walk to the right point Rancho San Carlos. Super-luxury resort.
Los Milagros Hotel Tel. 718-928-6647 (US), 011-52-624-143-4566 www.losmilagros.com.mx	Moderate+	All, Cable TV	Cash, Paypal	Pool Wifi	Cabo San Lucas. Good choice for quiet and cleanliness. Slightly off the beaten path. Some kitchenettes. Recommended.
Mar de Cortez Hotel Tel. 800-347-8821 (US), 831-663-5803 (US) www.mardecortez.com	Moderate	All, No TVs	Yes	Restaurant Bar Pool Parking lot Wifi	Cabo San Lucas. Great in-town choice for location and value. Good size rooms. Right across the street from Splash and Mermaids. Tours and massage services. Satellite TV in the bar. Recommended.

Marisol Boutique Hotel Tel. 011-52-624-142-4040 www.marisol.com.mx	Moderate/ low	A/C, Satellite TV		Pool Wifi	San José del Cabo. Near the beach midway between Zippers and Estero. Suites with ocean views. Each has 2 beds and a small refrigerator. Continental breakfast included. Nice, non-touristy choice.
Meliá Cabo Real Tel. 800-866-436-3542 (US), 011-52-624-144-2222; www.meliacaboreal.com	MUY expensive	A/C, Cable TV	Yes	Restaurants Bars Pool Spa Golf Wifi ($)	All-inclusive resort. Part of the upscale Summit Hotels & Resorts chain. On the beach at the Rancho San Carlos point.
Mira Vista Beach Condos Tel. 800-524-5104 (US)	Expensive	A/C, Cable	Yes	Pool	San José del Cabo. Quiet 1br condos on the beach at Zippers. All with terraces and beach views.
Misiones del Cabo Resort Tel. 888-745-2226 (US) www.hotelcabo.com/Resorts/mis iones.html	Expensive to muy expensive	All, Cable TV	Yes	Restaurant Bar Pools Tennis	Condo rentals sitting right on top of Monuments. Full kitchens and private patios.
Mykonos Bay Resort Condos Tel. 604-484-8488 (US), 011-52-624-142-3789 www.sea-side.com/mykonos.htm	Muy Expensive	A/C, TVs	No	Pool Jacuzzi Tennis Gym Wifi	Condo rentals near San José del Cabo right on top of Zippers. Full kitchens. Washer/dryer. Everything. Be sure to ask if for wifi as not all condos have it.
Posada Real Hotel Tel. 800-448-8355 (US), 011-52-624-142-0155 www.posadareal-hotels.com	Expensive	A/C, TVs	Yes	Restaurant Bar Pool, jacuzzi Fitness center Wi-fi	San José del Cabo. On the beach mid-way between Zippers and Estero.
San José Inn Tel. 011-52-624-355-3310	Cheapest!	No, Some TVs	No		Youth hostel In San José del Cabo.
The Mexican Inn Tel. 866-434-3467 (US), 011-52-624-143-4987 www.themexicaninn.com	Moderate	A/C, TVs	Yes	B&B	Bed & Breakfast in Cabo San Lucas. 3 blocks from the marina. Breakfast included.
Tropicana Inn & Bar Tel. 011-52-624-142-1580 www.tropicanainn.com.mx	Expensive	A/C, Satellite TVs	Yes	Restaurant Bar Pool	San José del Cabo. Continental breakfast included.
Westin Regina Tel. 800-WESTIN1 (US), 011-52-624-142-9000 www.westin.com	MUY expensive	A/C, Satellite TVs	Yes	Restaurants Bars Pools Spa Golf Gym Tennis	Cabo Corridor at Km 22.5. A lot of money to spend to have to drive to surf, but the wow factor for the wife or girlfriend will make up for your long drives to the East Cape. Bragging rights: The most expensive hotel ever built in Mexico. Balconies, phones, in-room safes—it's all here.

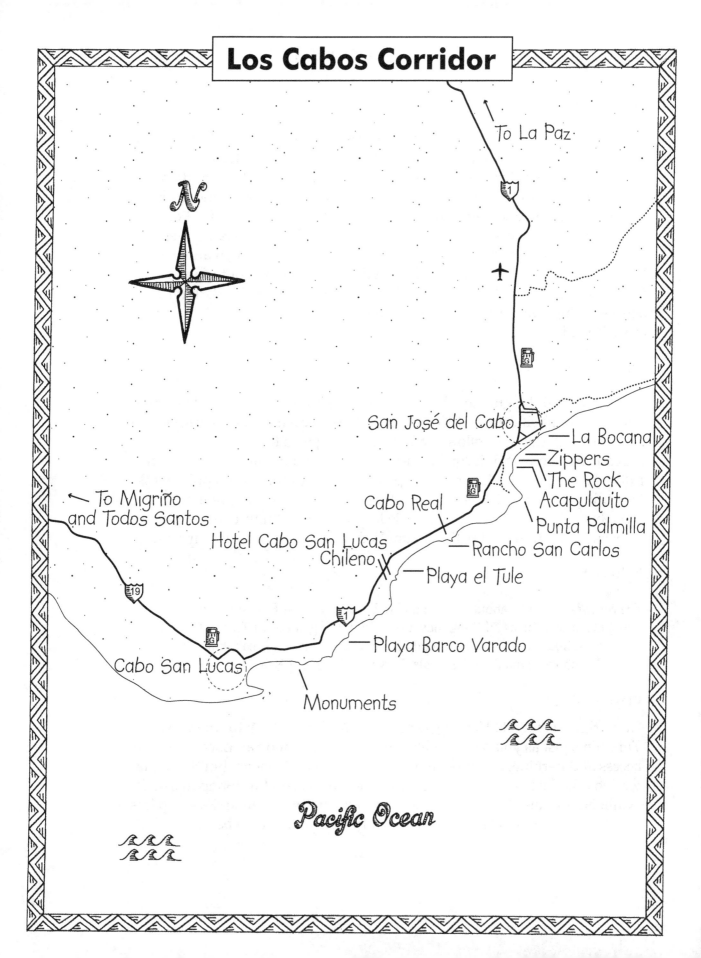

Los Cabos Corridor

To La Paz

N

San José del Cabo

La Bocana
Zippers
The Rock
Acapulquito
Punta Palmilla

To Migriño
and Todos Santos

Cabo Real

Rancho San Carlos

Hotel Cabo San Lucas
Chileno

Playa el Tule

Playa Barco Varado

Cabo San Lucas

Monuments

Pacific Ocean

Monuments

Powerful, rocky, left reef/point breaking just below and west of Misiones del Cabo condominiums on the west side of Cabo Bello, the eastern end of Bahía San Lucas. It's the closest break to Cabo San Lucas. Great shape and breaks even when the swell is small. Pull into the Misiones driveway and park just outside the gates to the right overlooking the trail to the break. Best on mid tide as low tide exposes lots of rocks and urchins. Also catches big west swells that wrap around Cabo San Lucas. You can stay in town and drive here in minutes, or rent a condo right at the break and slip out of your (expensive) bed into the surf. There is also the El Arco Trailer Park right across the highway, a bit of a walk to the surf. It's a point, so it doesn't handle crowds well.

Playa Barco Varado

One of the popular guidebooks speaks of a right pointbreak near the Cabo del Sol Hotel and golf course at Km-9. To get to the beach turn into the Sheraton Hacienda del Mar and follow the "La Playa" signs to the public beach. The beach is backed by a golf course and private development. It is a rocky reef-riddled stretch of beach with a few possibilities, but there is no pointbreak. One thing's for sure, it's not crowded. This writer is pretty sure that guidebook as somehow confused this location with Shipwrecks, as the name translates to "stranded boat", and applied the "right point" description.

Bahía Chileno

The Surf Report talks about a "right and left reefbreak just E of and in view of the Hotel Cabo San Lucas." I think they are really talking about El Tule, which is just west of the hotel. Bahía Chileno really is not much of a surf break, but it's a nice public beach frequented by the locals. Playa Chileno is at Km 14.

Playa El Tule

Good right reefbreak. Heading east at around Km-16 look for the Playa El Tule signs just as you pass Chileno and the Hotel Cabo San Lucas. Easy beach access and parking. Some say this used to be called Chileno, but the name was changed when the signs went up. The Costa Azul Surf Shop map calls it "Chileno 'El Tule'." Rarely crowded and usually pretty good. Picks up lots of swell. Blows out quickly from west winds. Camping on the beach.

Rancho San Carlos

The Surf Report says there is a right reefbreak here, between Km-19 and 20. The Moon guidebook says the same thing, referring to it as Playa Cabo Real. Unfortunately, the whole stretch around Km-19 and 20 has been developed into the Cabo Real resorts. Beach access is difficult. But no matter, there really is not much ridable surf in this stretch anyhow.

Playa Buenos Aires

Here's another one. The Moon guidebook says there is surf at Playa Buenos Aires. Once again, it's difficult access. And once again, good luck in finding this stealthy reefbreak at Km-22.

Punta Palmilla

AKA La Punta. Right breaking reef/point just below the Hotel Palmilla Resort between Km28 and Km29. Only breaks on really big swells, *really big,* or as the Costa Azul Surf Shop surf map says, "only over 20 ft. waves." You can probably park just to the east of the point by pulling in to where the sportfishing boats are parked. There is no surf there, which makes it a good channel to get out. The surf's way out around the point. Frankly, this writer isn't certain it's a right, as he's never seen it break, has never spoken directly with anyone who has actually seen it break, and has yet to see a verifiable photo of it.

Costa Azul

North of Punta Palmilla (yes, you're heading north now, but you have been for awhile now) is a bay with the three most frequented breaks in all of Baja Sur — Acapulquito, The Rock and Zippers. Pull over into the viewpoint to check out all three breaks. The Rock is right below the viewpoint, with Acapulquito to the southwest and Zippers viewed from the back to the east. Costa Azul is also the surf center for Baja as it's where you will find the best surf shops south of Ensenada, like the Costa Azul Surf Shop and Zippers.

Playa Acapulquito/Old Man's

The first Costa Azul break when driving southwest to northeast is a somewhat mushy reefbreak with mostly rights. Best on mid tide. Also called Old Man's, probably due to the longboard crowd, and the old men. Turn in at the big "Cabo Surf" sign and park in the lot (yes, it's the hotel's parking lot, or that of the 7 Seas Restaurant – good luck!) right in front of the break. Or drive on over to Zippers and walk back up the beach. Sand beach with rocks just as you step into the surf as with all of Costa Azul, so look before you leap. Stay at the Cabo Surf Hotel and not only can you walk to the surf but you can join the surf peanut gallery patio looking out over the break. And you'll have a parking spot.

The Rock

The middle break between Acapulquito and Zippers just below the viewpoint. Easy to find as there is always a bit of a crowd there, along with a giant rock—smaller ones too. It's a reefbreak that breaks mostly right. Needs a south or southwest swell, as with this whole area. Pay attention to the exposed rocks.

Zippers

The most famous and most crowded of all Cabo breaks – possibly in all of Baja, rivaling even San Miguel. Fast and fun right reef/pointbreak that is also loaded with locals who turn on the bad vibe as needed. Probably worse than the vibe is the fact that they really have the place wired, making it even more difficult to snag a wave. No matter, it's an excellent wave with less of a paddle than The Rock or Old Man's. Rocky at low tide. Parking just east of the break at the big sandy wash area south of the bridge. Heading east from the viewpoint over Acapulquito, take the next turnoff to the right down the hill. Or just head to the spot between Km28 and Km29. You can't miss it. You can rent surfboards right there on the beach in front of the break at a palm-thatched hut labeled (guess what) "Zippers."

San José Rivermouth/La Bocana/Estero San José

Good, juicy, hollow rivermouth/beach break east of the Holiday Inn Resort Hotel (formerly El Presidente Inter-Continental). Best when the summer *Chubascos* cause the estuary to overflow into the ocean (yuk) forming hollow sandbar barrels that pound. It also needs a south or southwest swell like the rest of the area. A local favorite, as the shop guys will tell you, and for good reason. The small crowds here spread out, so it's much more mellow than the Costa Azul spots. Best access is from the hotel or just west of the hotel. This is the last surf spot before heading to the East Cape.

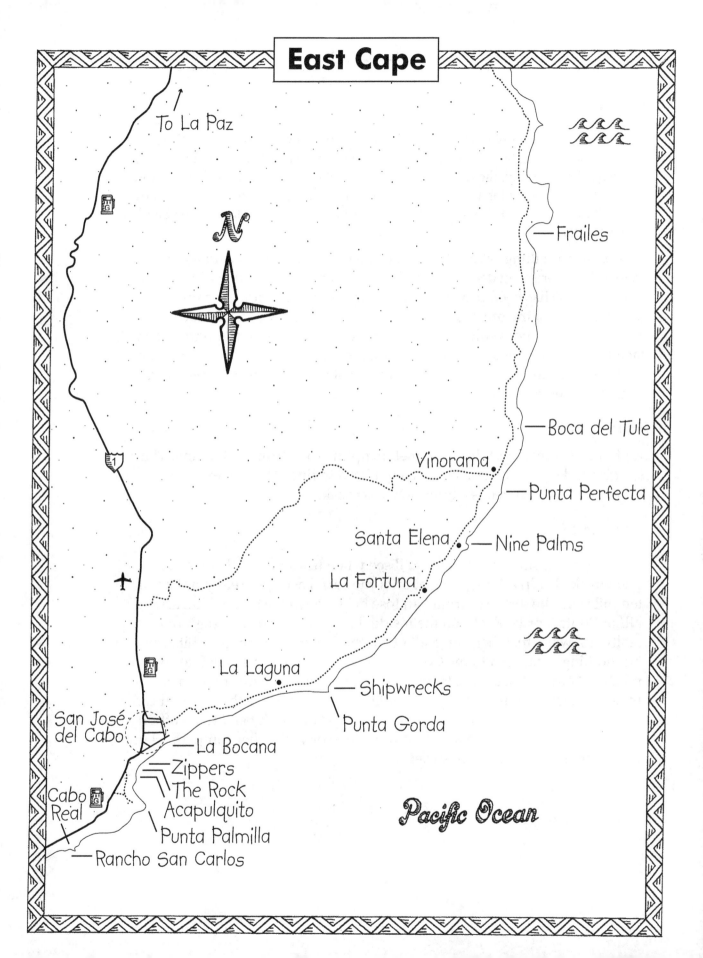

East Cape

To La Paz

Frailes

N

1

Boca del Tule

Vinorama

Punta Perfecta

Santa Elena

Nine Palms

La Fortuna

La Laguna

Shipwrecks

Punta Gorda

San José del Cabo

La Bocana

Zippers

The Rock

Acapulquito

Cabo Real

Punta Palmilla

Rancho San Carlos

Pacific Ocean

East Cape

Once you leave San José del Cabo heading east you are on the East Cape. Give yourself lots of time, have a full tank of gas and bring water. There is not much out this way. Drive through the San José del Cabo hotel district, make a left just before you get to the Holiday Inn (you will not; you will hit the dead end) then make a right at the circle heading off on the road that runs through the estuary toward the San José del Cabo Marina.

One of the nice things about the East Cape is that the surf is usually bigger than at the more crowded Corridor breaks. More importantly, while much of the East Cape has been privatized, limiting access, you can still camp on the beach at most of the breaks, which you can't do in the Cabo Corridor. But since the East Cape is still somewhat remote, there are few campgrounds with facilities, and the hotels that are here are mostly up around the cape to the north past where the surf usually breaks. Water temperatures range from the mid-60s to the mid-80s.

Punta Gorda

Right reef/point about three kilometers up the road from La Laguna. The spot is marked on most maps so it's not hard to find. The waves are a different story as it needs a huge swell to break.

Shipwrecks

Likely the first surfable waves you'll see when heading out the East Cape. The wrecked ship is long gone, but not the surf. Fast right reef-point about ten miles up the dirt road from San José del Cabo in the Santa Cruz area just NE of Punta Gorda. Rocks on the inside that get covered with high tide. It is a really fun wave that picks up a lot of southerly swell. It can get a bit crowded, but nothing compared to the Costa Azul spots. There is also a left at the northeast end of the bay. Lots of good surf in this area—mostly right-breaking reefs—all the way up to Punta Perfecta. The nice thing is you can see the breaks from the road all along here, so you don't need to go off on excursions (yet). Lots of places to camp, alone or with other campers. Many if not most of the campers are surfers.

Where to Stay for the East Cape

Lodging Name	Rates	A/C, TV	Credit Cards	Facilities	Comments
Maxey's at Shipwrecks Fax.011-52-114-82787 Email: ajnj@concentric.net	Moderate	No	No	B&B	One room with one bed and a patio. 5 minute walk to beach. Includes breakfast. Meals available on request.

Nine Palms

We call it Nine Palms. The Mexicans call it Santa Elena, or Rancho Santa Elena. One of the most popular East Cape surf spots, Nine Palms is a long right point wave featured in many of the videos seen of this side of Cabo. Good waves with good shape even if a bit mushy. Nine Palms is a more forgiving wave, especially on high tide, so some call it a longboarding wave, but it's really a fun performance wave with long rides for surfers of all types and levels, depending on size, of course. Can hold shape up to double overhead, maybe more. Rocks out near the lineup. Needs a good south swell.

Around Rancho Santa Elena look for the palm trees. There are more than nine, but a bunch of palm trees in this stony desert really stand out, so you can't miss it.

Punta Perfecta

Perfecta is a right reef/point that gets powerful and barrels with size. Not for beginners. Needs a strong south swell and can get a bit crowded. The wave can be difficult to see from the road, especially if you are driving up from the south, but if you drive south from Vinorama you can catch a glimpse of it from the main road. There are two ways in. Find the dirt road just north of Rancho Los Amigos, park on the cliff and hike down (leaving your vehicle defenseless), or drive in to Vinorama and onto the beach to the south. It's basically about a half-mile south of the Crossroads Country Club, a beachfront restaurant and bar that's also the local expat hangout. Eat on the beach; live music on Saturday nights.

This whole area and north is pretty amazing, as south swells come up and wrap all the way around to the west, and into these famed long, right, sandbottom points.

Boca del Salado/Boca del Tule

To the north is Boca del Salado, and to the south near the lighthouse is Boca del Tule (another "Tule"). All along this stretch up to Los Frailes you will find a bunch of breaks, depending on the swell – sandbottom right points and reefs. But it needs a lot of swell for waves to start breaking up this far. Access to Boca del Salado easy as it's a wide rivermouth delta where you can drive right up to the beach, assuming you have a beachworthy vehicle.

Frailes South

Some beach- and reefbreaks, but the truth is, from here north the Sea of Cortez does a pretty good imitation of a lake. Swells need to be strong out of the southeast or very strong souths for this area and north, or generated by local Sea of Cortez storms. *The Surf Report* reports shark attacks here.

Los Frailes

Left reefbreak near the small, upscale hotel. Camping at north end of the bay.

Where to Stay

Lodging Name	Rates	A/C	Credit Cards	Facilities	Comments
Bahía Los Frailes Hotel Tel. 800-934-0295 (US), 011-52-624-145-1332 www.losfrailes.com	Muy Expensive	Yes	No	Restaurant	Cottages and suites right on the beach. Rates include three meals. Deep sea fishing arranged. Kayaks rented.

Cabo (Bahía) Pulmo

About five miles north of Los Frailes, the coastal road dips down close to the beach at Bahía Pulmo, a shallow bay stretching from Pulmo Point on the north end to Los Frailes on the south. The only living coral reef in western North America fans out in seven or eight major reef fingers from the beach in front of the Cabo Pulmo Beach Resort, a quiet beach village with bungalows and casitas. Excellent diving (divers report seeing hammerheads), good little restaurants, and a nice little ex-pat community are just a few of the features of this protected national marine park beach. The park itself runs about five miles from Playa Las Barracas in the north to Los Frailes in the south.

There is a whole variety of breaks in this stretch, from reefbreaks to beachbreaks, but it needs very strong south swells, the more southeast the better. Also takes the north Sea of Cortez swells. Once again, though, it's inconsistent up this far north.

Heading north from Cabo Pulmo through to Rancho Leonero, signs of life grow further apart.

Where to Stay

The Cabo Pulmo Beach Resort bungalows are studios with kitchens. All are steps from the beach. The rentals are privately owned and furnished, giving each its own character and style. All accommodations include weekly linen change but no daily maid service. For more info call 1-888-99-PULMO or email cpbr@primenet.com. There are also campgrounds here with showers as well as RV parking. Check with the dive shop for other places to stay.

Lodging Name	Rates	A/C, TV	Credit Cards	Facilities	Comments
Cabo Pulmo Beach Resort Tel. 888-99PULMO (US) 011-52-624-141-0244 www.cabopulmo.com	Moderate to expensive	No	Yes	Tennis Dive center	Ranging from bungalows to a beach house, all with kitchens. SCUBA, kayak rentals
Villa & Casa del Mar Tel. 888-225-2786 (US)	Muy Expensive	All	No		Houses on the beach for rent

Little Arena

When it gets really big from hurricane swells, and the southern tip and breaks further south are big, closing out or out of control, head up here. Little Arena is a sandy point/beach break just south of the "big" Punta Arena. It picks up swells from both the south (but they better be strong swells) and the more infrequent north swells generated by Sea of Cortez storms. Do not bother heading into the El Rincón settlement; it's private and there is no Rincon there anyhow.

Punta Arena

Long, sandy, remote, easternmost point of the Baja peninsula with waves breaking on both sides, depending on the swell direction. The left point break is better. While most of the swell comes from strong souths that wrap into the gulf, local storms up the gulf also produce waves in this area. Take the turnoff at Las Lagunas (not to be confused with La Laguna near San José del Cabo). It is a long way out there.

Punta Colorado

If you have lots of time, or are not really on a surf trip but want to get way away from it all, you might want to check into the Hotel Punta Colorado. There is a reef in front of the hotel that breaks only occasionally and only from swells generated by local storms in the Sea of Cortez. Easy to find by following the signs to the hotel starting at the paved road that connects La Ribera with Las Lagunas. But if you decide to leave the main dirt road leading to the hotel, you are likely to get lost, and for no good reason as there is not much surf around here, or anything else. And it's tempting because you can see the Punta Arena lighthouse from the hotel.

Where to Stay for Punta Colorado

There is really only one place, the namesake hotel. Or you can head a bit north to the Rancho Leonero, which is actually in a nicer area.

Lodging Name	Rates	A/C, TV	Credit Cards	Facilities	Comments
Punta Colorado, Hotel Tel. 877-777-TUNA (US) www.vanwormerresorts.com	Expensive	A/C	Yes	Restaurant Bar Pool Airstrip	Price includes three meals daily. Totally geared toward fishing.
Rancho Leonero Resort Tel. 800-646-2252 (US), 760-634-4336 (int'l) 1-141-0216 www.rancholeonero.com	Very expensive	A/C	Yes	Restaurant Bar Pool	Fishing resort. Not very fancy for the price, but it includes three meals daily. Some ocean view patios. A bit of a drive to any surf. It is pretty much a lake out front.

Where to now?

If you have been driving up the East Cape from the south you probably haven't surfed since passing Punta Perfecta or Tule. And if you have driven the whole way from the California border down, you now need to make a choice: Either turn around and head back—surfing the whole way, of course—or head to Mainland! You aren't far from La Paz, where you can take the ferry across the Sea of Cortez to more uncrowded surf, cervezas, and trunking it the whole way. Vamos amigos!

INDEX TO MAPS

APPENDIX

Book List

Goth Itoi, Nikki, *Baja*, Berkeley, CA, Moon Handbooks, 2009

Baja California Almanac, Las Vegas, NV, Baja Almanac Publishers, Inc.

Baja California Road Log, Updated 8th Edition, San Ysidro, CA, Instant Mexico Auto Insurance Services, 2000

Goring, Jeremy et al., *Wave-finder Mexico*, London, United Kingdom, Hedonist Surf Company, 2006

Higginbotham, Patti and Tom, *Backroad Baja,* Sparks, NV, Somethin's Fishy Publications, 1996

Kelly, Neil and Kira, Gene, *The Baja Catch,* Valley Center, CA, Apples and Oranges Publishers, 1998

Mexico's Baja California, Automobile Club of Southern California, Costa Mesa, CA, 2001

Niemann, Greg, *Baja Legends*, Sunbelt Publications, 2002

Peterson, Walt & Michael, *Exploring Baja by RV,* Berkeley, CA, Wilderness Press, 1996

Lonely Planet Baja California 5th Edition, Victoria, Australia, Lonely Planet Publications Pty Ltd, 2001

Potter, Ginger, *Baja Book IV,* El Cajon, CA, Baja Source, Inc., 1996

Renneker, Mark et al. *Sick Surfers Ask the Surf Docs & Dr. Geoff,* Palo Alto, CA, Bull Publishing, 1993

Williams, Jack & Patty, *The Magnificent Peninsula,* Redding, CA, H.J. Williams Publications, 1998

Travel Agencies and Services

BAJA ACCOMMODATIONS, 800-800-9632, www.gobaja.com

BAJA AIR VENTURES, 800-221-WAVE, www.bajaairventures.com

BAJA SURF ADVENTURES, P.O. Box 1116, San Marcos, CA 92079, 800-HAV-SURF

Car Rentals

ADVANTAGE RENT-A-CAR, Cabo San Lucas, 011-52-114-3-0909, www.advantage.com

AVIS, Phone 800-331-1212, 800-331-1084, 011-52-146-0201 (San José del Cabo), 011-52-143-4607 (Cabo San Lucas), www.avis.com

BUDGET, Phone 800-472-3325; www.drivebudget.com

CALIFORNIA BAJA RENT-A-CAR, Phone: (619) 470-RENT, Toll Free (888) 470-RENT, www.cabaja.com

DOLLAR, Phone 800-800-4000, www.dollar.com

HERTZ, Phone 800-654-3001, www.hertz.com

THRIFTY, Phone 800-847-4389 (US), 011-52-624-143-1666 (Cabo San Lucas), 011-52-142-2380 (San José del Cabo), 011-52-146-5030 (Los Cabos Airport), www.thrifty.com

Mexican Consulates

Florida, 305-441-8780

Los Angeles, 213-341-6818
New York, 212-689-0456
San Diego, 619-231-8414

U.S. Consulate

Tijuana, 011-52-664-622-7400, or 619-692-2154 (U.S.) for emergencies after hours

Highway Help

Angeles Verdes (Green Angeles), from anywhere in Mexico 8am-8pm, tel. 01-55-5250-8221
Infotur, from anywhere in Mexico 24hrs, tel. 01-55-5250-0123

Surf Shops & Ding Repair

Baja Surf Center, Ensenada
Cabo Surf Shop, San José del Cabo @ Km. 28, 858-964-5117 (U.S.), 011-52-624-172-6188 www.cabosurfshop.com
Costa Azul Surf Shop, San José del Cabo, 011-52-624-142-2771, www.costa-azul.com.mx
Inner Reef Surf Shop, Rosarito @ Km. 34.5, 011-52-661-6132065
K-38 Surf Shop, Carretera Libre Ensenada-Rosarito, Km. 38 El Morro, 661-614-1009, www.k38surf.webs.com
Killer Hook Surf Shop, San José del Cabo, BCS, Mexico; tel: 011-52-114-2-2430
Pescadero Surf Camp, Km 64 on Hwy 19 between Cabo San Lucas and Todos Santos, Barrio las Palmitas, Pescadero, BCS, Mexico; fax: 011-52-612-134-0480; www.pescaderosurf.com

San Miguel Surf Shop, Ensenada
Todos Santos Surf Shop, La Paz Airport, La Paz, B.C.S, Calle Degollado y
    Cuauthemoc in Todos Santos, Playa Los Cerritos, Km 64 Hwy 19
Tony's Surf Shop, Blvd. Juarez, Rosarito, 011-52-661-2-1192

Surf Camps and Tours

Baja Surf Adventures. Surf trips to Northern, Central and Southern Baja.
    www.bajasurfadventures.com
Mag Bay Tours, 271 Magnolia, Suite B, Costa Mesa, California, 800-599-8676, 949-
    650-2775, www.magbaytours.com
Ojo del Huracan Todos Santos Surf Trips, La Jolla Beach Camp, Punta Banda, #66G,
    tel. 619-954-9798 (U.S.), 011-52-646-154-2753 (Mex), email
    ojodelhuracan@yahoo.com
Pescadero Surf Camp, K-63+, Barrio las Palmitas, Pescadero, BCS, Mexico; Tel.
    800-847-5921, fax 011-52-114-50288, www.pescaderosurf.com

Other Information and Web Sites

www.AllAboutCabo.com – A city guide for Cabo San Lucas
Baja Bound Mexican Insurance: www.bajabound.com
Baja Destinations: www.bajadestinations.com
Baja Life Online: www.bajalife.com
Baja Links: www.bajalinks.com
Baja Nomads online travel club: www.bajanomads.com
Baja Norte State tourism office: tel. 011-52-668-19492
Baja Quest: www.bajaquest.com
Baja Times biweekly newspaper: www.BajaTimes.com
Baja Travel Resource Guide: www.escapist.com/baja
Baja Web: www.baja-web.com
Baja.com/The Interactive Peninsula: www.baja.com
Baja4fun: www.baja4fun.com
Bing Maps: www.bing.com/maps
Ensenada Baja California: www.ensenada.com
Discover Baja Travel Club: www.discoverbaja.com
Google Earth: www.google.com/earth
Los Cabos Guide: www.loscabosguide.com
Magic Seaweed: www.magicseaweed.com
Maps: www.surfmaps.com, www.maplink.com, www.surfermag.com,
    www.bajaalmanac.com, www.mexicomaps.com, www.mapquest.com
Mexican Embassy in the U.S.: www.embassyofmexico.org

Mexinsure Insurance: www.mexinsure.us
MEXonline: www.mexonline.com
Mexico tourist information: tel. 800-44-MEXICO
www.mexicomaps.com
Oceanweather: www.oceanweather.com
Rosarito Style: www.rosarito.org
Scorpion Bay: www.scorpionbay.net
Surf.Baja.Com: www.surf.baja.com
Surfbreak Rentals: www.surfbreakrentals.com
Surf-forecast.com: www.surf-forecast.com. Great website with specific information
    for spots not covered in other sites
Surf-Mexico: www.surf-mexico.com
Surfing in Mexico: www.surfinginmexico.com
Surfline: www.surfline.com
SURFTV.com global internet surf directory: www.surftv.com
The Surfer's Guides: www.TheSurfersGuides.com
TodosSantos-Baja.com (not the island): www.todossantos-baja.com
WetSand surf reports and forecasts: www.wetsand.com

INDEX

MY BAJA NOTES

MY BAJA NOTES

CPSIA information can be obtained
at www.ICGtesting.com
Printed in the USA
BVHW062330040123
655552BV00017B/62